GETTING INTO OLYMPIC FORM

OLYMPIC FORM

THOSE WHO KNOW TELL WHAT IT TAKES

GETTING INTO OLYMPIC FORM

THOSE WHO KNOW TELL WHAT IT TAKES

Thomas D. Fahey, Ed. D.

Foreword by Al Oerter
Photographs by Wayne Glusker

Butterick Publishing

ACKNOWLEDGMENTS

Photographs on pages 17, 20, 23, 40 (both), 50, 60, 94, 95, 100, 111, 112, 116, 117, 121 (right): *Wide World;* pages 44, 49: *Focus On Sports;* page 69: *Globe.*

Library of Congress Cataloging in Publication Data

Fahey, Thomas D
Getting into Olympic form.

(A Butterick good-time fitness book)
Includes index.
  1. Olympic games. I. Title.
GV721.5.F33   796.4'8   79-29706
ISBN 0-88421-073-1

Book design: Arthur Ritter, Arthur Ritter, Inc.

CONTENTS

FOREWORD

A child comes to know at a very early age whether he or she has a special physical talent that makes him or her somewhat unique in a peer group. This talent, expressed as uncommon speed, strength, or balance, will normally form the basis of early acceptance within the group and provide the first understandings of self. It makes little difference that this talent is displayed by being able to run faster, lift heavier objects, or move with more grace; the talent provides a continuing source of enjoyment and as such is exercised time and time again.

These first enjoyable experiences, enhanced by years of training, competition, and thought for those who choose to do so, may result in one of the most intense experiences people can undertake: Olympic competition. The journey toward the Olympics is both demanding and rewarding, at times the most confusing and enlightening—and for some the most threatening—experience of an athlete's life.

The text of *Getting Into Olympic Form* describes in terms we can all understand the mental and physical profile of the Olympic athlete. Many of the techniques Olympians use to enhance their athletic performance are presented, but no attempt is made to define the ideal combination of training considerations as this will always be based on the needs of the individual athlete. In the past, perhaps twenty years ago, the training methods of Olympians consisted primarily of intense repetitive effort confined to the sport participated in, but this has changed dramatically. Today's athlete works harder in other areas that complement the sport, rather than devoting all time to the sport itself. As an example, a discus thrower must be concerned with additional strength through a well-defined weight-training program, a flexibility program to enhance movement within the throwing ring, balance work usually attained through some form of gymnastics, precise analysis of throwing motion by computer, imagery visualization, mental rehearsal, etc., as well as actual throwing. How these considerations become part of an Olympian's program (and the type of person who chooses to become an Olympian) is discussed with respect to several individual athletes.

Athletes' Olympic performances follow them the balance of their lives through countless introductions, conversations with friends, and private moments of thought. If the athlete prepared well for his or her Olympic moment, these thoughts will always be of a time when they put themselves on the line and, in that environment, learned a great deal about themselves. How and why they came to be a part of that special place called the Olympics is the subject of the following text.

Gold medalist Al Oerter (left) and Ben Plucknett size up their competition in the discus throw.

1
THE OLYMPIC MYSTIQUE

"The Olympics are magic," said Bruce Jenner, gold medal winner in the decathlon at the 1976 Olympic Games. "It's difficult to describe the excitement, the pageantry, and the electricity in the air at the Games. The feeling of having thousands of people in the stadium and millions of television viewers cheering me on was exhilarating beyond belief. The interest, the pressure, and the expectation are incredibly intense; they make the Olympic Games the most unique sporting event in the world."

The mystique of the Olympic Games lies in their uniqueness and their common appeal. Any sport that's universally played is represented at the Games. Every season, sports such as soccer, track and field, basketball, and gymnastics attract a fanatical following all over the world. But the Olympics bring everything together for one huge world championship — once every four years. For spectators, the Games become a symbol of national pride as the world's greatest athletes assemble to compete against each other in one arena. For world leaders, the Olympics often represent a political tool that can be manipulated for propagandist purposes. And for the athletes themselves, the Games represent the peak of excellence and the object of a lifelong dream: the one opportunity to prove they are the best at what they do.

Ultimately, all of the politics, bickering, and nationalism take a back seat to the competition itself. Only the athletes can comprehend the real magic of the Olympics, for only they know how the competition actually feels. And this special knowledge is for most athletes an end in itself, an intangible privilege that looms larger than winning or losing, as aptly described by Theodore Roosevelt: "Far better it is to dare mighty things, to win glorious triumphs, even though checkered by failure, than to take rank with those poor spirits who neither enjoy much nor suffer much, because they live in the gray twilight that knows neither victory nor defeat."

Gold medalist Bruce Jenner racked up 8,618 points in the decathlon at Montreal to set a world, American, and Olympic record. Here he exhibits his Olympic form in the shot put, one of the ten events in the two-day contest.

Although many people have difficulty relating to the vast ideological and philosophical differences among the many nations represented at the Games, the event of the Olympics provides the opportunity for people to meet on the common ground of sports. The thrill of victory and the agony of defeat are emotions everyone understands, and nowhere are these more intense — or more final — than at the Olympics. Achievement at the Games is clear-cut: an athlete or national team either wins or loses, and that is that. There is no tomorrow in the Olympics; the chance to improve a losing performance at the next Games is four years into the future — a lifetime away.

"I was involved in a desperate struggle against the best athletes in the world," said Bruce Jenner. "My performance was the end result of a lifetime of training and the embodiment of all my hopes and dreams. I was at the peak of my abilities and I had one shot at making sports history. The alternative was retiring into obscurity. The Olympics set a high price for victory; weakness of the body or weakness of the spirit spells defeat. It's 'do or die' when the competition begins. The Games are the supreme test of the athlete."

Olympic fame often escapes top athletes who are widely successful except at the Games, and this detracts from the public image of their greatness. Notable examples are Karl Schranz, Dutch Warmerdam, and Ron Clarke. Each of these athletes clearly dominated his sport, but lacked the gold medal victory that leads to athletic immortality. Schranz, the great downhill skier from Austria, was always overshadowed by gold medalist Jean-Claude Killy. When Schranz's chance for the gold came during the 1968 Games, he was declared a professional and barred from competition. Dutch Warmerdam dominated the pole vault during the 1940s, at a time when World War II prevented the staging of the Olympics. Warmerdam's athletic feats were compared to those of the legendary Jesse Owens, yet his lack of success in the Olympics tarnished his luster. Ron Clarke, perhaps the greatest distance runner of all time, was also a victim of circumstances. His chance for Olympic fame came in the 1968 Games, in the high altitude of Mexico City. Clarke was beaten by men who lived and trained at high altitude — athletes whom he easily defeated at sea level.

If the Olympic Games were an annual event, each of these men would have clearly dominated his competition. But by design, the Games are staged at four-year intervals — once each Olympiad. (In ancient Greece, where the Games originated, the equivalent of one calendar year was roughly a four-year period as we know it. The time span between each celebration of the Olympian Games was known as an *Olympiad*. In modern language, the Olympiad is the quadrennial staging of the Olympics.) Because the Games occur so infrequently, they are the focus of tremendous competition and worldwide attention unlike those in any

Jenner: "A lifetime of training "

other single sporting event. The uniqueness and appeal of the Olympics have resulted in the development of a special class of people, the Olympians. Whether they compete in track and field, skiing, swimming, or any of the other Olympic sports, the Olympians are alike in their single-minded dedication to the Games.

What does it take to achieve Olympic form and attain success at the Games? The Olympians are affected by pressures from their government, the press, and their fellow countrymen. These factors, along with their own self-generated pressures and drives, make the process of becoming an Olympian what it is. Although the nature of these pressures is different among athletes from various countries, the biological and psychological tools required for success in the Olympic arena are the same. To win a gold medal in the 100-meter butterfly, for example, a swimmer must have the prerequisite strength, skill, and psyche; buildups in the press, idolization at home, and extensive national support mean nothing if the athlete doesn't have what it takes when he or she hits the water. Outside pressures are factors in performance, though, and they are reflected in the competitive condition of the athletes at the Olympics. Internal and external pressures alike combine to shape the drives and motivations that keep an athlete training and competing.

The Meaning of the Olympic Games

Today, the Olympics are big business. The Montreal Games in 1976 cost $1.2 billion. For the 1980 Summer Games in Moscow, the television rights alone cost $85 million. And in September 1979, the American Broadcasting Company won the rights to provide exclusive coverage of the 1984 Games in Los Angeles with an incredible bid of $225 million; the total cost of broadcasting the Games on television will exceed $325 million. Because of the overwhelming popularity of the Olympics with consumers, many corporations spend tremendous sums of money to have their names associated with the Games. Coca-Cola, for example, spent more than $15 million for the right to have its famous soft drink designated the official drink of the United States Olympic team in 1980. As the Olympic Games continue to grow as an enterprise, their popularity swells larger and larger. What is behind the Games that holds such an enthralling fascination for so many millions of people? Understanding the mystique of the Olympics lies in knowing their importance to society and to the athletes themselves.

Part of the appeal of the Olympics for athletes and nations lies in the power of the Games to affirm a positive identity. The search for identity has been with man since ancient times. In the classical writings of Homer, for instance, the measure of a man was his name, his lineage, and his deeds. These identified the person and imparted security and a sense of worth. The warrior with an important family name and many victories was held above other men and considered unique. The drive for identity can be seen, on a smaller scale, in any children's playground. Children look up to the fastest runner, the best wrestler, and the most skilled ball player. Although the admiration for the physically skilled is sometimes consciously suppressed in the adult, it remains with each of us in the pit of the psyche. One of the great drives of man is to be special; instinctively, we admire the person who excels.

Top U.S. high-jumper Dwight Stones, two-time bronze medalist, leaped to a world record in 1976 by clearing the bar at 7 feet-7¼ inches.

Today family lines and traditions are less distinct, but the need for identity and uniqueness is still strong. Sports gratify these needs for many people. Most fans experience sports vicariously, and athletic achievement is often a vehicle of strong identification — when one's favorite athlete or team performs well in competition, one feels proud of the accomplishment. In the spectator's mind, the athletes in competition are an extension of the self.

The universal appeal of the Olympic Games gives them a special meaning within the context of man's search for both individual and collective identity. When a small country wins an unusual number of medals, for instance, the people of that country naturally feel that they hold a special place in the hierarchy of mankind: the proven superiority of their athletes reflects what they see as their own uniqueness and superiority. Because of the great number of nations represented at the Olympics — and because the Games receive worldwide attention — people from all across the globe can take pride in their athletes' accomplishments.

A strong athletics program has a positive effect on a nation's image. Communist governments understand this principle, and work to implement it. This represents a fundamental philosophical difference between Eastern-influenced and Western nations. Communist countries such as Russia, Cuba, and East Germany spend lavish amounts of money on sports programs that systematically develop children from a young age, and emphasize national athletic achievements to the people of the world. In the West, sporting prowess is held in high esteem because of the culture's basic respect for individual accomplishment. Communist countries, on the other hand, hold up their athletes as symbols of the strength of their political system; athletic success is prized primarily because of its positive effects on society. This policy was discussed by cultural journalist Hedrick Smith in *The Russians* (Quadrangle/New York Times Book Company, 1976): "Big-time sports in the Soviet system are not entertainment, as in the West, but politics, which is one reason why Soviet sports are so thoroughly subsidized and why top performers are secretly provided extra perquisites and handsome cash bonuses, especially for gold medal showings abroad. Sports champions, so goes the party line, prove the superiority of Soviet socialism. It is no accident that the Soviets are often the ones who seize every opportunity at the Olympic Games or other international competitions to insist on playing national anthems, displaying national flags, or performing march-pasts and other rituals that cater to national feelings and keep aflame the Soviet sense of patriotism and national pride."

The United States has only a modest program for Olympic development, yet the mystique of the Games remains strong. Our competitive drive in many Olympic sports is fierce even without massive financial support from the government. Leni Johnson, an Olympic swimmer from Norway, trained in the United States at the DeAnza Swimclub in California. "Swimming in America is much more competitive than in Europe," she said. "Kids only eight to ten years old are already grooming themselves for the Olympics. The practice sessions are longer and very intense. There's a heavy emphasis on winning, and this has a lot to do with the success of the American swimming program."

The Olympics provide athletic men and women with a rare opportunity to exhibit extreme physical and psychological courage. In this context, the Games reflect a struggle that is basic to human nature: survival of the fittest. However, the Olympics are also tainted by the frailties of human nature. Because of the tremendous universal significance of the Games, athletes and governments sometimes violate the noble ideal on which the Olympics were founded by using the Games as a rostrum for political statements. Arbitrary decisions are often made on the basis of political interests rather than athletic ones, and judging in sports is sometimes biased according to nationalistic considerations outside of the competition. Many people in the sports world feel that the United States basketball team was shamelessly deprived of a gold medal in the

PREMIERE SWIMMERS OF THE U.S. WOMEN'S OLYMPIC TEAM

Kim Peyton, a key member of the 1976 team that captured the gold in the 400-meter freestyle relay with a record Olympic mark of 3 minutes-44.82 seconds.

1972 Games in Munich because of biased judging. And in Olympic sports such as gymnastics and diving, unjustifiably differing scores between Western and Communist judges are commonplace.

Over the years, a few political interest groups have used the Games toward their own ends and completely distorted the meaning of the Olympics. The results have often been shocking: Hitler's political exhibition at the Berlin Games in 1936; the symbolic personal statements by American athletes at Mexico City in 1968; the withdrawal of 24 African nations from Montreal in 1976; and, most horrifying of all, the murder of eleven Israelis at the Munich Games in 1972.

The athletes themselves are sometimes guilty of violating the spirit of the Olympics by taking unfair advantage of their opponents. Some Olympians have been caught taking drugs, such as amphetamines and anabolic steroids, to boost their performance. Illegal practices like blood doping, heating bobsled runners for greater speed, and even assaulting opponents have been the focus of intense controversy at the Games.

The Olympics are an exhibition of the human species at the peak of its athletic potential, honed to a fine edge to produce top performances. In spite of the intense rivalry, the frequent political undercurrents, and the

Olympian Jo Harshbarger (center) has held many American records in the freestyle.

Shirley Babashoff won one silver medal in 1972 and four in 1976, and anchored the team gold medal in the 400-meter freestyle relay in both those years.

handful of crooked participants, the Games represent a means of improved relationships and understanding among people from many nations. Ultimately, individual accomplishments by athletes loom larger than the petty designs of political groups — or any other outside influence — who seek to distort the true meaning and ideal of the Olympics. Perhaps the best example occurred in the 1936 Games in Berlin, sometimes called the Nazi Olympics. Adolf Hitler hoped to use the Games to demonstrate his theory of Aryan supremacy. But Jesse Owens, a black athlete from the United States, put a crimp in the Fuehrer's plans. Owens captured the gold medal in the 100-meter dash and was favored to win the broad jump (now called the long jump). Unfortunately, Owens fouled his first two jumps and was in danger of being eliminated from the competition. But his chief rival, a blonde, blue-eyed German named Lutz Long, helped Owens with his steps in full view of 90,000 partisan German spectators. As a result, Owens survived the preliminaries and went on to win the finals with a jump of 26 feet-5⁵/₁₆ inches. Owens also won the gold in the 200-meter run, and anchored the first-place U.S. team in the 400-meter relay. The Nazi "master race" theory was shattered before Hitler's eyes.

The Olympics never will be — and probably never can be — completely consistent with the noble ideas on which they were founded, as stated by Baron Pierre de Coubertin in 1896: "The most important thing in the Olympic Games is not to win but to take part, just as the most important thing in life is not the triumph but the struggle." The news media will always tally the gold, silver, and bronze medals won, and nations will inevitably try to distort the meaning of the Games with political propaganda. But none of this can overshadow the striving for perfection in competition, or the opportunity provided by the Games to see man at his athletic best. Individual performance is all that really matters. The true spirit of the Olympics remains unchanging: to applaud great effort, regardless of who the athletes are and what they believe in.

The Olympians

"For a girl to become a top gymnast today she must train at least four hours a day, six or seven days a week, twelve months a year," said Alla Sversky, coach of the Los Angeles Gymnastic Club and Master of Sports in Russia. "A young gymnast can't afford a vacation — she has to stay in shape all year long. The tricks required these days are too difficult and the competition is too severe for her to do anything else. Sports demand total dedication and discipline. A young gymnast must begin formal training by the time she's eight years old. She will know if she has a chance to make it by the time she's ten."

Roger Bannister, the first man to run the mile in under 4 minutes, only trained about an hour a day before he set his record. Today his workout would be considered a light day to a high school athlete. In 1979, almost thirty years after Bannister's record, ten men finished a single race in under 3 minutes-55 seconds — times only 4 to 10 seconds faster than that first sub-4-minute mile. Yet those athletes are essentially full-time runners. Present-day athletic competition requires countless hours of training even for miniscule improvements.

Jesse Owens (center) wears the victor's oak-leaf laurel crown after winning the broad jump in 1936. Germany's Lutz Long (right) placed second.

Nadia Comaneci captured three gold medals in gymnastics at the Montreal Olympiad, and led her Rumanian team to a silver medal. In each of her medal-winning individual performances, she scored more points than any other female gymnast in Olympic competition.

The price for success in the Olympic Games is becoming greater and greater. An athlete must be developed into a human machine if he or she expects to be at all competitive. Decades ago, Jim Thorpe burned up the track with a minimum of preparation. But these days, dedication to Olympic athletics is a full-time job. The drive for excellence is emotionally and physically draining. As the Games become more and more competitive, there's tremendous pressure on the athletes to endure more pain, push themselves harder, and become further alienated from their families.

Success in women's gymnastics, as Alla Sversky said, requires experience in movement and dance before age eight. Then years of relentless training follow in an attempt at Olympic stardom. If a young girl has the right body structure — small and lean — along with exceptional talent and the good fortune of a delayed puberty, she may have a chance. But she must also have the money for the right coach, and in competition she must please the judges. Gymnastics is a sport where subjective impressions mean everything.

The legendary Jim Thorpe, a superbly talented natural athlete, won the decathlon and pentathlon at Stockholm in 1912, but was later disqualified when officials discovered that he had played professional baseball. His amateur status has been restored by Olympic officials.

A distance runner can expect to put in two-a-day workouts, covering 80 to 150 miles a week. The training will also include miles of exhaustive interval training that saps the energy from already fatigued muscles and greatly increases the risk of injury. The Olympic-caliber runner walks the edge of the sword that separates physical breakdown from peak performance.

A prospective ski team candidate is expected to drop out of a normal lifestyle and follow the snow. The racer's life may include a special school at a ski resort, summers in the snow in South America, and winters spent following the race circuit throughout the world — all in a desperate attempt to stay in top condition.

THE OLYMPIC EXPERIENCE: PERSONAL VIEWS

Judy Reeder-Calpin was a swimmer on the 1964 United States Olympic team. In the following years, Judy has been a swim coach, a student of sports medicine, and a physical education teacher. She has had time to put her Olympic experience into perspective. "I swam for the Santa Clara Swim Club and had teammates like Don Schollander and Donna deVerona," Judy remembered. "We were the top club in the world — it was almost a foregone conclusion that we would win if we entered a meet. At the time, I couldn't appreciate the severity of the workouts. I just accepted them as a way of life. I think I almost believed that all kids grew up that way.

"People say that competitive swimming puts a crimp in your social life. I don't think that's true. I became very good at budgeting my time. I eliminated such things as watching television in the afternoon like the other kids, but I was better off. I tended to have swimming friends, which I suppose had its negative points. But we always had a lot of fun.

"After the Olympics my life changed dramatically. People treated me a lot differently at school. It was easier to get dates and everybody knew who I was. I instantly had more self-confidence and I became more outgoing, something I'd never been before. Looking back, I feel the experience was healthy and positive. At the time, I often resented the pressure to win, but that's an innate requirement of big-time swimming. There is a price to pay — you spend half your life in a semi-fishlike existence. I probably missed a lot, but I had some very unique experiences."

Gold medal decathlete Bruce Jenner has similar feelings about his years of dedication to training: "The vast majority of athletes love the process of sport. I love competing — striving to improve, working desperately to be better than I am now. Even though training was painful at times, I felt that I was living life to the fullest. I knew that few people had the opportunity to live like I did, and that I might never have that opportunity again. I felt that I was developing myself to my highest potential — it was a great feeling."

The exhilaration of sport was described by miler Roger Bannister in his autobiography *First Four Minutes* (Putnam, 1955), as he reminisced about one of his early running victories: "I had expressed something of my attitude in life in the only way it could be expressed, and it gave me a thrill. It was intensity of living, joy in struggle, freedom in toil, and satisfaction at the mental and physical cost. It gave me a glimpse of the future because I had discovered my gift for running — an unconscious conspiracy of mind and body that made this energy release possible."

Most athletes are drawn to the Olympics to participate in the ultimate sports contest, but some are enticed by the mystique of the Games. Tom Dooley was on both the 1968 and 1972 American Olympic teams as a 20-kilometer race walker. "I am in love with the Olympics," Dooley said. "The spirit of the Games is part of me. Much of it is the tradition — the Olympics are one of the few institutions that have survived so long. Their roots go back into antiquity. In the days of the Greeks, wars were even stopped so that the Games could be held. That spirit of tradition has continued into the modern Games, to a certain extent. I remember the opening ceremonies at Mexico City in 1968: every conceivable effort was taken to make the Olympics a success, and that was the feeling that seemed to be held by everybody. People at the Olympics — the competitors, the officials, and the Mexican government — saw the Games as almost a holy pilgrimage. It was fantastic.

"The Olympic ideal has dominated my life, " Dooley added. "I compete because I've found something I'm good at, but that's only a small part of it. The process of amateur sport has given me the opportunity to compete when and where I want. It has kept me healthy and young. I always have a positive outlook on life. The Olympics made me think of life as a series of challenges. Part of the magic of the Games is that they represent the ultimate man-to-man competition. I have carried this spirit into my life — I accept challenge and I feel that I am a better person because of it. I try to do my best in everything I attempt."

Dooley is keenly aware of nationalistic pride at the Games. "A big thrill for me has been to represent my country in the Olympics," he said. "The feelings that I had during the opening and closing ceremonies made me very proud. I am grateful that I had the chance to travel throughout the world representing the United States."

Sports certainly offer great opportunities for adventure. There is a certain exhilaration in competing before large crowds, in meeting new people, in exchanging souvenirs with other athletes, and in traveling to foreign countries. "The athletic community is very special," said Bruce Jenner. "I have developed friendships with people all over the world that never would have occurred without sports. Seeing the world as an

Roger Bannister of Great Britain, first man to run the mile in under 4 minutes: "Joy in struggle, freedom in toil"

athlete is much different than seeing it as a tourist. When you visit a foreign country as a sportsman you're not a stranger, but a part of the sports world. You don't have to speak the same language because every athlete knows the language of sports. We all get along extremely well."

John Powell, American Olympian in the discus throw, said that the opportunity to travel provided a continuing lure to compete. Powell has competed in nineteen foreign countries and feels he's learned a lot about life along the way: "Competition and training have helped me relate to people, and have even helped me to like myself. At first I saw my competitors merely as opponents. In time I saw them as human beings. The competition didn't end at the conclusion of the meet, but continued

U.S. discus thrower Mac Wilkins set a world record in 1976 with a titanic toss of 232 feet-6 inches.

to act as a common bond among all the athletes. I like all my opponents and wish them well. When I compete against Mac Wilkins, I want him to do his best. If I beat him, then it's much more satisfying. Through my travels and experience, I've learned that the real battle is with myself, and not my competitors. The other athletes merely establish the criteria I use for improving myself."

Wilkins, one of the world's premiere discus hurlers in recent years, set a world record with an incredible throw of 232 feet-6 inches. Although his toss of 221 feet-5 inches in the 1976 Games was considerably shorter, the mark bested his closest opponent's by more than 4 feet and copped Wilkins the gold medal. He described his thoughts on competition in "Discus" by Ernie Bullard and Larry Knuth (L.K. Publications, 1977): "My philosophy has always been to do the best I can do to come as close to my potential as possible. I would always try to compete against myself. If I was a 170-foot thrower, it would be futile to measure my success by how often I beat a 200-foot thrower. Now that I have thrown 232 feet, what is the satisfaction of beating a 200-foot thrower if I throw 202 feet?

"No matter what my level of achievement, the greatest satisfaction always comes from competing against myself. What more can a person do? Everyone has different abilities, which are finite resources. The only thing that is not predetermined is how well we develop our resources.

Olympian Bruce Kennedy
nailed the 1977 AAU
National Championship
in the javelin throw with a
sling of 262 feet-3 inches.

This is the real challenge to me, not throwing a school record, 200 feet, a world record, or winning an Olympic gold medal.

"Discus throwing is currently my means of expressing myself and living the life I feel is best for me. During my college days I came to the conclusion that the important thing in life is not so much what you do, but how you do it. For me there is only one way — to the best of my ability. If you have a resource and the desire to develop this resource, you should do so to the utmost of your ability. I always ask the question, 'Is there anything more that I could possibly do to improve myself?'

"Many people feel that the sacrifices required to reach the top in any specialty are tremendous burdens. I don't look at my dedication to sport as a sacrifice or a harsh self-discipline depriving me of what I really want. What I really want is to do the things that will bring me closer to my maximum effort. It is a sacrifice for me to break my training routine."

For many athletes, sports provide a way of asserting themselves. Ron Laird, the great race walker from the United States, saw athletics as a way of improving his confidence. He wanted to be good at something, and he discovered that he could be good at race walking if he worked hard. "I wasn't big enough or coordinated enough to play football or basketball," Laird remembered. "I tried distance running, but I just didn't have the speed to excel. Then I discovered race walking.

"I started walking in the late 1950s, at a time when the sport was like a cult. People would honk their horns and throw rocks and bottles, trying to knock the walkers off the road. When I started, I was so embarrassed about the weird style required in race walking that I trained after dark so nobody would see me. As I became more confident, I didn't care what people thought. Gradually I got better and better, and I started breaking records. During my career, I've set 82 American records. Race walking has really given me confidence and a sense of self-worth: I'm not just another face in the crowd — I'm Ron Laird, the race walker."

Laird recalled the culmination of his years of training, when he put his self-confidence to the task: "My greatest moment in race walking was in 1971 at the Lugano Cup meet, the world championship of race walking. No American had ever done anything in that race. To do well, I knew that I would have to keep pace with the Russians, who were then the leading walkers in the world, no matter what. The Soviets went out at a ferocious pace, but I was determined to hang on. I said to myself, 'There's no way I'm going to lose contact with those guys.' I felt my muscles dying, and I thought surely that I was doing myself great harm. But I just kept going. I pushed myself harder than I ever had before, all the way to the brink of my endurance. I won the bronze medal in the competition. The winning wasn't important; it was the fact that I put myself to the ultimate test. I pulled out the stops and gave it all I had.

Olympic race walker Ron Laird has set 82 American records.

"Part of the appeal of the Olympics, " Laird continued, "is that there are thousands of athletes giving it everything they have at the same time and place. The Games are the one competitive event that means a lot to every athlete. In ordinary competition or even in a championship meet, you sometimes have athletes holding back or just going through the motions. But Olympics are the one meet that everybody peaks for — everyone is up and ready to do his or her best."

Rick Early, 1972 Olympian in diving from the United States, stressed the importance of the Olympics as a symbol of success: "I participated in diving because it was something I was good at. I didn't achieve instant success — I had to work very hard to make it. In college, I was only the third-best diver on the team. I became more proficient because I kept competing longer than most divers. Even though the Olympiad is the big meet, it really isn't the toughest competition. Because each country is allowed only three competitors, many of the world's great divers are eliminated from the Games. While the Olympics may have twenty top competitors, a meet like the United States National Championships may have thirty top divers. But the Olympics receive all the publicity, so there's more pressure to do well."

Many athletes feel that athletics taught them to know themselves. It's pretty difficult to put yourself to the limits of endurance without learning something of your mettle. Don Schollander, who won an unprecedented four gold medals in swimming at the Tokyo Games in 1964, expressed this in his autobiography, *Deep Water* (Ballantine Books, 1971): "Was it worth it — working like hell, giving up so much — to get into that cutthroat world? Yes. Even without the medals and acclaim I won, it would have been worth it. You get so many intangibles out of swimming: discipline, confidence, experience. Whenever I lost I would ask myself why I lost — whether the reason was some weakness in myself. In swimming, you're alone a lot in the water with time just to think, and because of that I feel that I've gotten to know myself well."

Other athletes take great pride in doing something well. Brian Oldfield, world record holder in the shot put, sees himself as an artist. "The shot put is an art form — it's the way I express myself," Oldfield said. "When I go through a perfectly executed put, I feel like poetry in motion. It feels fantastic when everything clicks the way it's supposed to."

Brian Oldfield's story is a tragedy. He is by far the best shot-putter in history, yet he's unable to compete in the Olympics because he joined the ill-fated professional track tour several years ago. As a rule, professional athletes are barred from Olympic competition. However, Oldfield continues to throw for the fun of it in local all-comer track meets. Even with no incentives he can produce world-class performances — simply because he loves what he does.

Another athlete who enjoys the nature of her sport is Norwegian swimmer Leni Johnson, silver medalist in the 1978 World Championships in the 100-meter freestyle. Watching her effortlessly cut through the water, it's easy to see why she likes to swim so much: she looks like she's having fun, even during her grueling workouts. "I swim for myself — it makes me feel good. I don't think about beating my opponents, I just swim as fast as I can. I get a tremendous sense of satisfaction out of swimming the way I do." At 22, Leni is old for a female swimmer. "I will retire from competition after the 1980 Olympics," she said, "but I will never give up swimming."

Other athletes emphasize winning. Two swimmers from the United States, John Simmons and Chris Cavanaugh, radiated raw animalism as they talked about the joys of competition. Cavanaugh said, "The Olympics represent the top and that's where I want to be. Making the Olympic team means that I reached the potential I knew I had." Simmons, who competes for Stanford University, doesn't dwell on the Olympics alone: "I believe that if you want something badly enough, you'll get it. The Olympics represent making it into a very elite club. I want to be as good as I possibly can be; if I achieve my goal, the Olympics will undoubtedly be part of that."

Willie White smashed the American record in the women's long jump at Melbourne in 1956 and landed a silver medal. She has competed at four Olympiads since then.

Soviet speedster Valery Borzov gusted to gold medals in the 100- and 200-meter dashes at the Munich Olympiad, but took just one bronze in the Montreal Games.

To the athlete, amateur sports and the Olympics mean achievement, improved self-image, travel, and friendship. Even though athletes are proud to compete for their country, the underlying motivation of all the athletes I talked to was intrinsic: personal pride and self-satisfaction are the best stimuli in the quest for perfection.

The Origin of the Games

The Olympics have their origins in ancient times. Legend has it that the Games were started by Hercules in celebration of a great victory. The competition consisted of a race with his four brothers: Ephimedes, Idas, Peoneos, and Lasos. The prize was an olive branch. Whether this is fact or fiction, the Games were part of the Hellenic sports heritage long before they were formalized and held on a regular basis.

Although the Greeks had a long history of athletic competition (see the *Iliad* and *Odyssey* of Homer), the recorded beginning of the Olympics was 776 B.C. Iphitos, King of Elis (wherein Olympia lies), established the Games at the behest of the Oracle of Delphi, who suggested that Olympian contests might please the gods and rid the country of a disastrous plague. Eventually, as the Games became a regularly staged event, an armistice from all warfare was·declared at each Olympiad, and athletes were allowed safe passage to the arena.

U.S. gymnast Kathy Johnson, 1978 All-around National Champion

The early Games consisted of one event, the *dromos*. This was a foot race of 192 yards, the length of the stadium. Eventually, the Olympic program was enlarged and conducted over a five-day period. The opening ceremonies and sacrifices to the gods occurred on the first day. On the second day a contest was held for the *ephibi*, the younger men. The ephibian competition consisted of the *dromos*, wrestling, and the pentathlon, a combination of track and field events and wrestling. On the third day began the adult competition, which consisted of the *dromos*; the *dialos*, which was two laps of the stadium; the *dolichos*, a long-distance race about 2²/₃ miles; pugilism, or boxing; wrestling; and pancratium, a brutal combination of wrestling and boxing. On the

fourth day were held the equestrian events, the pentathlon, and the race with armor. The closing ceremonies, proclamation of the winners, and final sacrifices were held on the fifth day.

Contrary to popular belief, there was no marathon in the ancient Games. The first 26-mile course was run in 490 B.C. on the plain of Marathon by the Athenian runner Pheidippides, who was bringing news of a Greek victory to the people of Athens. Unfortunately, he didn't get the opportunity to improve his time — he died at the end of the run.

Training for the ancient Games became more rigorous with time. This, no doubt, occurred for the same reason as it has today: the uniqueness and tradition of the Olympics grew stronger, and made the Games more

and more competitive. Specific training schedules were designed to take place in the gymnasium, a special place designated for the training of Olympians. Athletes were expected to train for ten months prior to the Olympic competition. Before being allowed to compete, they had to swear that they were physically prepared and that they would play the Games fairly, a stipulation that remains in the modern Olympic oath.

The prize to the victor in each contest was an olive wreath cut from the sacred tree of Hercules. The winners were practically immortalized: statues of their likenesses were sculpted by Greek masters and placed in the sacred grove of Jupiter at Olympia. Heralds would sing of the victors, their parents, and their country. The winning athletes were also given a lifetime pension, and their reentry into their home city was made through a breach in the wall — much more dramatic than going through the gate.

The Olympics were a very important part of Greek civilization. They served as a source of cultural identity for the Greeks, even during the Roman Empire. The celebration of the Games was a kind of religious festival that involved music and drama as well as sports — activities the Greeks believed gave pleasure to their gods. However, just as in modern times, the greatest appeal of the Games was entertainment: the assembly of the finest athletes in the land for tremendous competition.

With the decline of the Greek city-states came a gradual decline in the Olympics. Participants became more and more professional, and corruption entered the judging. In 394 A.D. the Games were abolished by the Christian emperor Theodosius, in an effort to suppress pagan rituals.

The Modern Olympic Games

The revival of the Olympic Games, in 1896, is credited to Baron Pierre de Coubertin, a French aristocrat. De Coubertin believed that peace among nations could only come with the development of good will among individuals, and that sports could help in the promotion of friendly relations among young people.

During the late nineteenth and early twentieth centuries, amateur athletics were the pursuit of gentleman sportsmen. Sports were played during one's leisure time. However, as athletes attempted to improve performances, more and more training time was demanded. Eventually, the intense, fanatical level of training became a prerequisite of all the Olympic sports.

The first modern Olympic Games were staged, appropriately, in Athens in 1896. The outstanding athlete in the competition was Robert Garrett of the United States, who won the discus throw with a toss of 95 feet-7 inches — even though he had taken up the sport only two weeks earlier. Garrett, captain of the Princeton track and field team, also won medals in the shot put, high jump, long jump, and standing triple jump — a feat that would be virtually impossible today. In contrast, Bruce Jenner had to train twelve years to win one gold medal at Montreal in 1976.

The Olympic motto is *Citius, Altius, Fortius* — Faster, Higher, Stronger, which aptly describes the progress of the athletes in the modern Games. Table 1 shows a comparison of performances in track and field for three Olympiads: Paris (1900), Helsinki (1952), and Montreal (1976). Since the early Games, and even since Helsinki, times and distances have undergone a tremendous metamorphosis. Most of the improvements can be attributed to new training methods and greater training intensity, along with better equipment and facilities.

TABLE 1
COMPARISON OF GOLD MEDAL PERFORMANCES
IN MEN'S TRACK AND FIELD EVENTS

Event	Paris, 1900	Helsinki, 1952	Montreal, 1976
100-Meter Run	10.8 sec.	10.4 sec.	10.06 sec.
200-Meter Run	22.2 sec.	20.7 sec.	20.23 sec.
400-Meter Run	49.4 sec.	45.9 sec.	44.26 sec.
800-Meter Run	2 min.-1.4 sec.	1 min.-49.2 sec.	1 min.-43.5 sec.
1,500-Meter Run	4 min.-6.2 sec.	3 min.-45.2 sec.	3 min.-39.17 sec.
5,000-Meter Run	—	14 min.-6.6 sec.	13 min.-24.76 sec.
10,000-Meter Run	—	29 min.-17 sec.	27 min.-40.38 sec.
Marathon	2 hr.-59 min.-45 sec.	2 hr.-23 min.-3.2 sec.	2 hr.-9 min.-55 sec.
110-Meter Hurdles	15.4 sec.	13.7 sec.	13.3 sec.
400-Meter Hurdles	57.6 sec.	50.8 sec.	47.64 sec.
3,000-Meter Steeplechase	—	8 min.-45.4 sec.	8 min.-8.02 sec.
400-Meter Relay	—	40.1 sec.	38.33 sec.
1,600-Meter Relay	—	3 min.-3.9 sec.	2 min.-58.65 sec.
Pole Vault	10 ft.-9 $9/10$ in.	14 ft.-11 $1/8$ in.	18 ft.-$1/2$ in.
High Jump	6 ft.-2 $4/5$ in.	6 ft.-8 $5/16$ in.	7 ft.-4 $1/2$ in.
Long Jump	23 ft.-6 $7/8$ in.	24 ft.-10 in.	27 ft.-4 $3/4$ in.
Triple Jump	47 ft.-4 $1/4$ in.	53 ft.-2 $9/16$ in.	56 ft.-8$3/4$ in.
Shot Put	46 ft.-3 $1/8$ in.	57 ft.-1 $1/2$ in.	69 ft.-$3/4$ in.
Discus Throw	118 ft.-2 in.	180 ft.-6 in.	221 ft.-5 in.
Hammer Throw	167 ft.-4 in.	197 ft.-11 in.	254 ft.-4 in.
Javelin Throw	—	242 ft.-0 in.	310 ft.-4 in.
Decathlon	—	7,887 pts.	8,618 pts.

THE OLYMPIC EVENTS

With the exception of track and field, swimming, basketball, boxing, and Alpine skiing, few of the Olympic sports receive much publicity or are even widely practiced in the United States. Americans have been successful in other Olympic sports largely because of individual initiative. This is not to say that the United States is not sports-conscious; but football and baseball are vastly more popular with Americans than any other sports.

The Olympic program is extremely diverse. In all, thirty sports are contested, with the competition divided into Winter and Summer Games. The hosting country at any Olympiad has the option of adding a nontraditional sport for those Games.

Archery

Target archery was part of the early Olympics until 1920, when it was discontinued. It was reintroduced at Munich in 1972. The competition spans four days and consists of 288 arrows shot from various distances.

Archery: The United States placed first in both the women's and men's competition at the 1972 and 1976 Olympiads.

The United States has dominated this sport, winning both the women's and men's gold medals in the 1972 and 1976 Games. But in spite of American success in archery, the survival of the sport in this country is threatened by underexposure.

Basketball

Basketball is a major sport in the United States. It is little wonder that the Americans have dominated the game in the Olympics since it was introduced in 1936 at Berlin. U.S. men have won the gold medal in every Olympiad except in 1972, when a disputed call resulted in defeat at the hands of the Russians. The major power in women's basketball is the Soviet Union. However, the game is becoming a major women's sport in this country and the United States should continue to improve. The American women's team won the silver medal in 1976 at Montreal.

Biathlon

Biathlon is part of the Winter Olympics and involves a combination of cross-country skiing and rifle sharpshooting. The three events in the sport include a 20-kilometer race, a 10-kilometer sprint, and a four-man relay. The sport is dominated by the Nordic countries and the Soviet Union. Although it has been a military-oriented activity, biathlon has not been actively supported by the United States Army. However, the biathletes are a dedicated group of competitors. According to Dr. Gene "Topper" Hagerman, director of the Sports Medicine Laboratory at the Olympic Training Center in Squaw Valley, California, "they probably have more physical and mental toughness than any other group we have worked with."

Bobsledding

Bobsledding is a Winter Olympics event involving races with either two- or four-man teams. The sled runs consist of a high-walled track with a series of steeply banked curves. Until 1956 the United States had dominated the event, but because of superior training facilities, the Europeans have taken over the lead.

Recently, the most prominent power in bobsledding has been East Germany. They introduced the concept of using big, fast men who could get an edge at the start. Previous strategy involved using smaller men who were more skilled at selecting the correct line on the course.

There is only one bobsled run in the United States, located at Lake Placid. Long-range plans call for the construction of other sites to make the sport more popular and accessible.

Women's basketball: The Soviet and U.S. teams finished first and second, respectively, in the inaugural women's Olympic competition at Montreal in 1976.

Before his world renown as Heavyweight Champion Muhammad Ali, Cassius Clay battled his way to the gold medal in the light-heavyweight boxing contest at Rome in 1960. Above: Clay throws a powerful right at Australia's Tony Madigan, who tied for the bronze with Giulio Saraudi of Italy.

Boxing

The boxing event is divided into weight-class contests that each consist of three 3-minute rounds. International-style boxing emphasizes defensive skills and finesse rather than the more offensive style popular with professionals. Club boxing is very popular in the United States, which largely accounts for American success in the sport.

American boxers tend to compete in one Olympiad and then turn professional. The most notable examples of former Olympians with successful professional careers include Muhammad Ali, George Foreman, and Joe Frazier. Communist boxers often continue in "amateur" competition, and are thus much better schooled in the intricacies of international competition than Americans.

Canoeing and Kayaking

These events consist of racing canoes and kayaks in flat water over distances ranging from 500 to 1,000 meters. There are fewer than 400 competitive paddlers in the United States, and canoeing and kayaking is a minor sport in the American Olympic effort. The events are dominated by the Rumanians, Russians, and Hungarians.

Cycling

Cycling has become the center of worldwide interest since the gas crisis of 1973. Although the Europeans dominate the sport, Americans are beginning to make progress in international competition.

Cycling competition takes place on the track and on the road. Distances in track events range from 1,000 to 4,000 meters. The races are run against the clock, in head-to-head sprints, or in team and individual pursuit. Pursuit races place riders on opposite sides of the track, the object being to overtake the opponent. Road races include a 100-kilometer team race against the clock and a 175-kilometer individual race.

Cycling: Modern Olympic events include the individual and team road races; the 1,000-meter scratch; the 2,000-meter tandem; the individual and team pursuits; and the 1,000-meter time trial.

Diving

Olympic diving consists of men's and women's competition in the 3-meter springboard and 10-meter platform. Divers compete both in preliminary and final rounds. Women perform ten dives and men eleven in each round. American divers have consistently dominated the competition, in spite of a small number of competitors and a sparsity of 10-meter platforms. Other world diving powers include Mexico, Sweden, Russia, East Germany, Italy, and Holland.

Equestrian

The equestrian competition pairs man and horse as a working team. The United States usually does well in this competition, and the sport is well organized in this country. There are three types of competition: Grand Prix dressage, Prix des Nations jumping, and the three-day event. Dressage involves a series of compulsory exercises performed in a ring that demonstrates the horse's control, obedience, balance, and suppleness. Jumping involves horse and rider negotiating a course over sixteen to twenty obstacles. The three-day event is a combination of dressage, endurance running, and jumping.

Fencing

Men compete in foil, épée, and saber contests, while women compete in the foil only. A foil is a flexible blade with a blunt point. The object of the foil competition is to touch the trunk of the opponent with the point of the blade. The épée is similar to the foil, but stiffer. A touch can be made on any part of the body. The saber is a cutting as well as slashing weapon. Touches occur above the waist and can be accomplished with the point or cutting edges.

The United States has never done well in international fencing competition, but interest in the sport in this country has grown in recent years. At present, fencing is dominated by Europeans.

Field Hockey

Field hockey is played with a ball and stick and is similar to ice hockey or soccer. In countries like India or Pakistan, field hockey is a major sport that engenders the kind of passion seen at South American soccer matches or American football games. Countries compete in regional matches before the Games in order to determine who will actually play in the Olympics. The United States has never excelled in field hockey competition. However, an effort to improve our standing, particularly in women's competition, is gaining momentum.

Equestrian sports: Horse and rider work as a competitive team.

Field hockey: International competition spotlights many female stars. The sport was developed in England during the mid-1800s.

Figure Skating

Figure skating is one of the more popular events in the Winter Olympics. There are four events: men's singles, women's singles, pairs, and ice dancing. The United States has dominated the singles events, while the Russians and East Germans tend to lead in the pairs and dancing.

Skating is a big-money sport requiring considerable resources for coaching, travel, and ice time. However, the chance to follow in the footsteps of Dorothy Hamill, Peggy Fleming, and Sonja Henie has attracted many young athletes to this sport.

U.S. gold medalist Dorothy Hamill displayed dazzling Olympic form in the figure-skating event at Innsbruck in 1976.

Soviet gymnast Nikolai Andrianov has collected five gold medals in Olympic competition, including the all-around individual in 1976.

Gymnastics

Gymnastics is another crowd-pleaser. Olga Korbut and Nadia Comaneci, stars of the 1972 and 1976 Olympics, have inspired people all over the world to take an interest in this sport. The men's competition has been dominated by Russia and Japan, while Russia and Rumania have headed the women's competition.

In the Olympics, men and women must compete in two routines in each event. Men's events are the long horse, side horse, horizontal bar, parallel bars, rings, and floor exercise. Women compete on the balance beam, uneven parallel bars, side horse, vault, and in floor exercise. Medals are awarded for individual events, all-around excellence, and team competition.

Ice Hockey

Ice hockey is an exciting, hard-hitting game that is very popular in the Winter Olympics. The sport is dominated by the Russians, Czechoslovakians, and Swedes. The Soviets have been playing together as a team for many years and are undoubtedly the best in the world. In 1979, they beat a team of professional all-stars from Canada.

Ice hockey is very popular in the United States. However, the American team has little opportunity to practice as a unit, and so it has difficulty in international competition.

Judo

Judo is a combative sport between two athletes who use throwing and grappling techniques to fell or subdue the opponent. Athletes compete according to weight classes. Judo was first included in the Olympic program in 1964, at the Games in Tokyo. It was dropped for the 1968 Olympiad, then reintroduced in 1972 at Munich. Japan has won the majority of the medals, although the United States has been fairly successful.

Luge (Tobogganing)

A luge is a small sled. Men's and women's competition takes place on a course similar to a bobsled run. There are no luge tracks in the United States; American lugers have had to train in Europe or on the bobsled run at Lake Placid. The 1980 Winter Games in Lake Placid should result in remarkable improvement in training facilities for American lugers, who, like their Canadian counterparts, have not fared well in the Olympics. At present, the luge is a European-dominated event.

Modern Pentathlon

Pentathlon is a military-oriented event consisting of riding a horse over a 1,000-meter course with obstacles, épée fencing, pistol shooting, 300-meter swim, and 4,000-meter cross-country run. Competitors are awarded points, which are tallied to determine the winner. The U.S.S.R., East Germany, and Hungary are the leading medal winners at the Olympics, although the United States usually puts in a credible performance. American pentathletes have one of the finest training facilities in the world at Fort Sam Houston, Texas.

Rowing

Rowing involves competition in sweeps and sculls. A sweep oarsman uses one oar, while a sculler uses two small oars. Olympic competition includes events with one, two, four, and eight oarsmen. There is separate competition for men and women.

Rowing: In 20th-century Olympic competition, the U.S. team has won eleven gold medals in the eight-oared shells with coxswain.

The United States has done exceedingly well in rowing, particularly in the men's eight-oared shells with coxswain. American women made a credible showing at the Montreal Games in 1976, the first year of women's competition. In recent years, East Germany has been the leading power both in men's and women's rowing.

Shooting

Shooting has been on the Olympic program since 1896. There are seven events, divided into rifle and pistol competition. The rifle competition includes small-bore (.22 caliber) prone and small-bore free, as well as clay-bird shooting and skeet shooting. The pistol competition includes both rapid-fire and free pistol shooting.

Although the shooting event is not highly publicized, the United States has done extremely well in Olympic competition. Other international leaders in this sport include Russia and Poland.

Skiing

Skiing is divided into Alpine and Nordic events. In Alpine skiing, men and women compete in the downhill, slalom, and giant slalom races. Men's Nordic events include the 15-, 30-, and 50-kilometer cross-country races, the 40-kilometer relay, the Nordic combined (ski jumping and cross-country racing), and 70- and 90-meter ski jumping. Women compete in 5-, 10-, and 15-kilometer cross-country races.

Alpine skiing has always been one of the glamour events of the Olympics. Skiing stars such as Toni Sailer, Stein Eriksen, and Jean-Claude Killy have used their Olympic victories as a springboard for commercial and financial success. Although the sport has been well financed in the United States, American athletes have had few victories in Olympic competition. However, the outlook is improving. Alpine skiing has been dominated by France, Austria, Canada, Switzerland, and West Germany.

The popularity of cross-country skiing is booming in America and Canada, and the United States won a silver medal in the 1976 Winter Games. World powers in Nordic skiing include the U.S.S.R., Finland, Sweden, East and West Germany, Czechoslovakia, and Switzerland.

Soccer

Soccer is by far the most popular sport in the world. Although not previously emphasized in America, it is the fastest growing youth sport in the United States. This should provide a base for future successes in the Olympic Games.

Countries must qualify for Olympic competition in a series of preliminary contests that involve over a hundred teams. Only sixteen teams make the final competition. The United States has made the final only once, in 1972, when it finished last. Olympic competition has recently been dominated by East Germany, Poland, and the U.S.S.R., although other teams from South America and Europe are also highly competitive.

Speed Skating

Men and women participate in speed skating. Men's events include 500-, 1,000-, 1,500-, 5,000-, and 10,000-meter races, while women skate distances of 500, 1,000, 1,500, and 3,000 meters.

The United States has been very successful in speed skating, winning thirty medals since 1924 — in spite of inadequate training facilities. Americans have been forced to train in Europe to stay competitive. Other top countries in speed skating include the U.S.S.R., Norway, Sweden, Holland, and East and West Germany.

France's Jean-Claude Killy swept the three Alpine ski events at Grenoble in 1968.

U.S. swimmer Mark Spitz completely dominated the competition at Munich in 1972 by sweeping seven gold medals and setting a new world record in each victory.

Swimming

Swimming is one of the center attractions at the Summer Games. Men and women alike compete in thirteen events divided into the following categories: freestyle, butterfly, breaststroke, backstroke, medley, and relay.

Over the years, American men and women have dominated Olympic competition in swimming. However, there have recently been strong challenges from other countries, notably East Germany and the Soviet Union. American men won 69 percent of all swimming medals at Montreal in 1976, while American women won only 18 percent — a dramatic decline from the 62 percent the women won in 1968. However, the renewed effort to strengthen the swimming programs in the United States should reinforce our standing in future Games.

Team Handball

Team handball, almost completely unknown in the United States, is a sport played indoors. The game is played with a ball six inches in diameter, and combines elements of soccer, basketball, and field hockey. There is separate competition for men and women. The leading teams are from the U.S.S.R., Rumania, and Yugoslavia.

Track and Field

Track and field is the center of attention in the Olympics. There are 24 men's events and fourteen women's events, including sprints, middle-distance and long-distance runs, hurdles, walks, jumps, vaulting, throwing, steeplechase and relay races, and the pentathlon and decathlon. Competition is becoming fierce, partly because of a worldwide fitness craze that took root beginning in the early 1970s.

Olympian Maren Seidler has held the U.S. record in the women's shot put.

The United States has traditionally dominated the competition in men's track and field, but other countries are etching away at our lead. Track and field has seen great stars from all the continents; except in a few events, no area of the world has consistently maintained a hold on a particular event. In addition to the United States, notable track powers include East Germany and Russia. U.S. women have not fared as well as the men, but with the upsurge of women's athletics in America, this situation will change.

U.S. hurdler Mike Shine (above) bounded to the silver medal in the 400-meter event at Montreal. Teammate Edwin Moses (right) took the gold in 47.64 seconds, a world, American, and Olympic record.

Volleyball

International volleyball is a fast game played by skilled and agile athletes — a long way from the Saturday-afternoon game in the front yard. As in soccer, teams play in regional tournaments for the opportunity to compete in the Olympics. Men and women participate in separate Olympic competition.

Although volleyball is increasingly popular in the United States, we have been unsuccessful in international competition. The U.S.S.R., Poland, Czechoslovakia, Japan, and Cuba have dominated men's volleyball, while Japan, U.S.S.R., and Korea have led the women's competition.

Volleyball: Men's and women's competition was introduced at the 1964 Olympiad in Tokyo.

Water polo: Top-level competition requires exceptional swimming speed and endurance, along with adroit ball-handling skills and brilliant strategy.

Water Polo

Water polo is played with a ball in a swimming pool. The rules of the sport are similar to those of soccer, or hockey — it's played with the hands. Water polo is fast and rough, and requires considerable teamwork.

Hungary, Yugoslavia, Russia, and Italy tend to have the best teams in this sport. Older athletes dominate water polo — the most successful teams have years of experience playing together. As in most other team sports, the United States team is hampered by the lack of opportunity to train as a unit. In addition, there is only regional interest in the sport — the entire United States Olympic team in 1976, for instance, was from California.

Weightlifting

The weightlifting competition in the Olympics involves two lifts: the snatch and the clean and jerk. Both require the use of two hands in lifting the weight. Athletes compete in classes according to body weight. Contrary to popular belief, these lifts require considerable quickness and explosiveness, not only brute strength.

The United States dominated the weightlifting competition until the 1960s. In 1976, Russia won 22 of 27 medals, while the United States won only one. Americans are hampered by lack of interest in weightlifting, while in Russia and Eastern Europe, the sport is big-time.

Wrestling

Olympic wrestling includes competition in freestyle and Greco-Roman events. Freestyle involves both lower- and upper-body holds, while Greco-Roman involves only upper-body holds. Wrestling is contested in weight classes.

Americans have done very well in Olympic freestyle competition, finishing second to Russia overall in 1972 and 1976, but the United States has never won a medal in Greco-Roman competition. Eastern European countries dominate both freestyle and Greco-Roman wrestling.

Yachting

Six of the thirty international racing classes are included in the Olympics. The class of a boat is determined by its size and design. Sailors compete on a specified triangular course. Each class races once a day for seven days.

The United States has traditionally done very well in Olympic competition. Other countries showing strength in yachting include England, Denmark, Russia, France, and Holland.

2
THE BODY

Who is the better athlete, the gymnast or the distance runner? Does the great strength of the weightlifter overshadow the blinding speed of the sprinter, or the endless endurance of the marathon runner? Is an athlete of Bruce Jenner's abilities superior to one of Jean-Claude Killy's, Wilma Rudolph's, or Jim Ryun's abilities? These questions are raised anew every four years, with the event of the Olympic Games. Yet no one has found definitive answers, and it's safe to say that no one ever will. Each sport demands a well-defined Olympic form, and each produces its own champions.

Getting to the Olympics requires a unique combination of two factors: training and genetics. In one area, the athlete has complete control of his or her level of success; in the other, he or she has none. To a large extent, Olympians are born and not made. They have the natural physical talents required for success. Without these inborn talents, Olympic-caliber performance is impossible — regardless of how much "heart" an athlete may have.

Athletes reach the Olympic level of physical prowess by combining their genetic abilities with years of hard training and dedication. Long and heavy training in any particular sport leads to specialization as the body adapts to the physical requirements of that sport. Sprint training, for example, develops the nerves and muscles for speed; the body improves its ability to generate large amounts of energy very rapidly. Distance running, on the other hand, requires a well-developed cardiovascular system so that the athlete will have great endurance; the body needs energy over a long period of time rather than all at once. In training for technique sports, such as figure skating and gymnastics, the athlete develops complex movement patterns that can be repeated flawlessly time after time. In these sports, control of energy is more important than the capacity to explode for a few seconds or endure for hours.

Soviet gold medalist Olga Korbut

Each Olympiad brings together a large group of extraordinarily talented athletes. In any of the events, participation alone represents a great athletic achievement: physical ability at its ultimate level of performance. The long process of athletic development begins with learning complex movement skills, and continues through arduous training to gain strength and endurance — and a shot at the gold. Yet without the genetic factors of ideal body composition and metabolism, that process cannot possibly culminate in Olympic form. Truly, the Olympians are gifted people.

Genetics and Athletic Performance

In recent years, sports scientists such as Paavo Komi of Finland and Vassilis Klissouras of Canada have taken great interest in the genetic contribution to athletic performance. Their research indicates that genetics is the most important factor not only in the determination of body structure, but also in the performance and characteristics of muscles and nerves. Successful athletes in any particular sport are comparable in physique, skill level, strength, and endurance. The significance of body structure in Olympic competition is obvious: basketball players, for example, are tall and lanky, while female gymnasts tend to be small and petite. Distance runners are usually less than six feet tall and very lean, while discus throwers are much taller and more muscular. If an athlete doesn't have the right build and training capacity for a particular sport, he or she isn't going to be successful at that sport.

It's not surprising that genetics is responsible for the performance of the nervous system in sports. The nervous system, comprised of the brain, the spinal cord, and peripheral nervous structures, has a far-reaching effect on the quality of athletic performance: it determines how fast muscles contract and how precise muscular movements will be. And because the nervous system is partly responsible for how quickly muscles fatigue, it is also important in defining the extent of the body's endurance.

Genetics also determines how quickly an athlete learns a sports technique and how well he or she will respond to training. A genetically gifted athlete can master basic movement skills rapidly, and then quickly begin working on the more complex skills and subtleties required in international competition. Olympic-caliber athletes are also quicker and stronger, and they can employ techniques impossible for the average person participating in sports on a recreational basis.

Because they respond to athletics differently than 99.9 percent of the population, top Olympians are actually biological freaks. Take Renaldo Nehemiah, one of the most talented athletes to burst onto the scene in

years. It has been speculated that Nehemiah is capable of holding the world record in five events: the high hurdles, the 400-meter hurdles, the 200- and 400-meter dashes, and the long jump. Athletically, Nehemiah is a world apart from the average person, and he was born that way. The first time he bowled, for instance, he rolled a score of 235. That certainly isn't the type of performance most of us turn in.

Russ Rogers, head track coach of Fairleigh Dickinson University, described Nehemiah's natural gifts in a recent newspaper interview. Rogers told of a drill he had conducted with Nehemiah and three other world-class athletes. Each athlete assumed the runner's position in the starting blocks, fingers on the ground. Proceeding down the line, Rogers held a soft-drink bottle 6 to 18 inches above each athlete's hand. He explained that when he dropped the bottle, the athlete should catch it; if the athlete could not react quickly enough, the bottle would land on his hand. "Most guys reacted just before the bottle hit the ground," said Rogers. "Nehemiah was reacting before the bottle was halfway down. You can't move any part of your body until your hands move. I've been using that drill for years, but I've never seen anyone handle it better than Nehemiah. And you can't teach that to someone."

Renaldo Nehemiah (left), top-ranked U.S. hurdler, may be capable of holding world records in five different events.

Jesse Owens: superb
natural talent

Perhaps the best example of an athlete with superb natural talent is the immortal Jesse Owens, who collected four gold medals at the 1936 Olympiad in Berlin. Owens's long-jump record of 26 feet-8¼ inches, set just before the Berlin Games, remained the best in the world for a quarter century — yet he had spent relatively little time training for the event. Dink Templeton, former Olympian and famed Stanford track coach, once commented on Owens's incredible abilities: "Put him in anything and give him enough work and he'd break every running record in the book up to two miles. Owens was such a gifted athlete that team duty—he was good for four firsts in any meet—kept him away from his sprint potential. Larry Snyder (Owens's coach from Ohio State University) never dared run Owens in time trials or extra work sessions in practice. After all, when you have a diamond you don't treat it like quartz."

Sports science has developed sophisticated selection processes that are now employed all over the world. Because of these, athletic competition will continue to grow tougher; genetically gifted athletes can be identified early in life and developed to their full potential. Gone are the days when a farmboy with tremendous raw ability could come out of nowhere to win the gold medal at the Olympics. Although it may be an attractive story line for Hollywood films, this kind of accomplishment is no longer possible. Participation in today's Games requires not only a wealth of natural ability, but a lifetime of back-breaking training.

The Physiology of Olympic Form

METABOLISM AND BODY COMPOSITION

The body is a lot like a machine — in order to move it requires energy. The successful athlete can produce and utilize large amounts of energy efficiently. Metabolism, the sum total of the chemical reactions occurring in the body, is responsible for the breakdown of food to provide energy to do work. The metabolism of the sprinter or the shot-putter has been adapted through training to provide large amounts of energy all at once. The metabolism of the endurance athlete, on the other hand, provides energy over a longer period of time.

The body composition of athletes — that is, the amount of body fat and fat-free weight they carry — is a critical consideration in the Olympics. In some sports, failure is imminent if an athlete carries too much fat. Excess fat on a distance runner would create the same effect around the track as packing a lead weight. On the other hand, if a female swimmer is overly lean, she may ride too low in the water and lose efficiency; in this case a certain amount of body fat is an advantage.

U.S. Olympian Francie Larrieu laps the 1,500-meter racecourse at a championship meet.

At the DeAnza Human Physiology Laboratory in Cupertino, California, we work each year with hundreds of people who are interested in assessing and improving their physical fitness. These people range from housewives and business people to world-class athletes. The performance characteristics of some of the athletes have been truly amazing — they are a breed apart from the rest of us. These athletes can perform physical feats that average people could never even hope to approach, no matter how hard they trained. One of the best examples of a naturally talented athlete I've ever seen is Bruce Wilhelm, 1976 Olympian in weightlifting. During his long athletic career, Wilhelm has been a world-class wrestler, shot-putter, and Olympic-style weightlifter. He could run a 100-yard dash in 9.9 seconds at a body weight of 270 pounds. In 1978, Wilhelm won the World's Strongest Man contest, which was presented on national television, by defeating other top athletes — weightlifters, bodybuilders, and professional football players. At the DeAnza Lab, shortly after the 1976 Olympics, Wilhelm weighed in at 350 pounds — but only 23 percent of that weight was fat. The average person his age (34) has between 18 and 21 percent fat. Considering Wilhelm's massive body weight, he was pretty lean.

Another amazing natural athlete is Brian Oldfield, a world-class record holder in the shot put who can also produce top competitive performances in the discus and hammer throws — events he doesn't even practice. At the DeAnza Lab, Oldfield measured only 10 percent fat at a body weight of 265 pounds. He was so powerful that he exceeded the capacity of the Lab's measuring devices, something that hadn't happened before and hasn't since.

Sports scientists have studied the body composition of many types of athletes. A comparison of average body composition in selected Olympic sports is shown in Table 2. In general, the percentages of body fat reflect the energy requirements of each sport and the sex of the athlete (women naturally tend to have more body fat than men). Sports with the highest energy requirements, such as distance running, result in very low levels of body fat — it's very difficult to run a hundred miles a week and be obese. In sports like synchronized swimming, with a lower energy requirement, the athletes' body composition is similar to that of the general population.

TABLE 2:
BODY COMPOSITION OF SELECTED OLYMPIC ATHLETES

Sport	Percentage of body fat	Sport	Percentage of body fat
BASKETBALL (men)	16.0	HURDLES	
DISCUS THROW		men	10.2
men	16.4	women	19.0
women	26.0	SHOT PUT	
DISTANCE RUNNING		men	16.5
men	7.0	women	28.0
women	15.2	SKIING	
GYMNASTICS		men	7.5
men	8.0	women	20.0
women	12.9	SWIMMING	
HIGH JUMP		men	12.0
men	10.5	women	16.5
women	19.0	WEIGHTLIFTING (men)	12.2
		WRESTLING (men)	9.8

The body structure of Olympians has changed since the early modern Games at the turn of the century. Dr. Robert Malina, an anthropologist at the University of Texas at Austin, notes an increase in body size among athletes in most sports. Modern athletes also tend to be larger than the average population. Dr. Malina hypothesized that this phenomenon is probably due to the increased competitiveness of the Olympics — larger people tend to be stronger and thus more successful at the Games. Also, the nature of the events in the Games has changed since the early years, and this has no doubt had an effect on the body structures of the competitors. In women's swimming, for example, there is a tendency toward more muscularity due to the new emphasis on building strength, along with the strenuous training schedule. Athletes in throwing events are becoming leaner because of an increased emphasis on speed and finesse, in addition to great strength.

Alla Sversky, the former Russian gymnastic coach who is now coach of the Los Angeles Gymnastics Club, discussed the body structure of female gymnasts: "She must have a small, powerful stature to perform the routines that win international competition today. You have to be born with it — all the training in the world is useless if you have the wrong shape. The tricks required today are physically impossible for the tall mature woman."

Sexual maturation seems to be delayed in many international-class female gymnasts. This gives them a valuable training edge — they can continue to improve their skills without the disadvantages of increased body fat and breast development that normally accompany womanhood. Rumors have circulated in the press that some of the top gymnasts have been given drugs to suppress their sexual development. Dr. Harmon Brown, hormone expert and chairman of the Olympic development committee for women's distance running commented, "I doubt if the Communist countries are giving their female gymnasts drugs to delay puberty. However, it is possible that the amount of protein in their diets has been restricted. Such a diet would tend to delay sexual maturation."

Techniques to correctly assess body fat and fat-free weight have been developed. The most accurate method available to the athlete is underwater weighing. In this test, the athletes are weighed with a scale that is suspended underwater. Fat is less dense and muscle more dense than water, and so the more muscular an athlete, the greater the underwater weight. This technique allows athletes to determine exact body composition and work to achieve the best balance between body fat and muscle. By comparing the energy expenditure through training with the energy uptake through diet, an athlete can attain an ideal body composition for his or her sport.

Success in women's gymnastics requires a small and lean body structure. Stretching exercises enhance flexibility and quickness of movement.

Soviet gymnast Olga Korbut won a pair of individual-performance gold medals at Munich in 1972, and a silver medal in 1976. In both those years, she was instrumental in Russia's typical gold-medal-winning team performance.

MOVEMENT SKILLS

Judging the quality of complex movement patterns in gymnastics, figure skating, or diving depends upon subtle differences in the execution of movements that appear almost identical. I remember watching the compulsory figures at the Broadmoor Ice Arena during the National Sports Festival in 1979. The skaters were expected to perform certain precise patterns on the ice. To my untrained eye, the performances were practically identical. Yet the judges were able to separate the competitors by large margins. In a technique event such as this, groups of talented athletes are separated by mistakes that may measure a fraction of an inch.

People who organize and process thoughts more quickly and uniquely than the majority of the population are labeled geniuses. Mental processes are nothing more than the transmission and organization of nervous impulses. These processes are very similar in accomplishing the complex movement patterns in sports. In a biological sense, superior athletes can also be called geniuses. Their natural talent is the translation of nervous impulses into the most efficient and economical movements required for their sport; the process from thought to athletic action is superior to that of the normal person. Using these criteria, a Jesse Owens or a Bruce Jenner has to be considered in the same category as an Albert Einstein.

Preparation for technique events in the Olympics involves years of practice to make very complex movements reflexive. Practice is aimed at eliminating negative aspects of motion and developing perfect execution of difficult and sometimes dangerous techniques. The trained eye of the coach is absolutely essential to this development. The coach must help the athlete translate motions that can be understood at a conscious level into subconscious actions.

Dr. Franklin Henry, from the University of California at Berkeley, was first to describe the development of sports reflexes. He called this process the *memory drum*. The precise patterns of movement are imprinted in the brain, much like on a magnetic disk in a computer, and can be recalled and performed by the athlete. The aim of practice and coaching is to ingrain the correct motion; if an incorrect motion is inscribed on the memory drum, the inappropriate technique will be executed during competition. The more an athlete practices a movement (up to a certain point on a learning curve, depending on the sport), the more it is reinforced on the memory drum. Therefore, it is imperative that the movement be as correct as possible. Henry discovered that the imprint on the drum was extremely specific — if the speed of the movement was altered, the execution of the movement would be much less precise. So the athlete must not only practice difficult movements, but execute them at the speed to be used in competition.

Athletes have used many techniques to improve the precision of the movements inscribed on their memory drum. Some use meditation, during which they see themselves performing each motion correctly. Others have tried self-hypnosis to help themselves feel the technique. Athletes also study loop films of top techniques performance to help them gain insights about execution and motion. New methods of "mental practice" are being developed that involve watching the same movement on videotape, hour after hour. However, the bottom line is practice — years and years of practice. Most technique sports require that the athlete begin serious training between eight and ten years old. Then he or she must put in four to six hours of practice a day, all year long. The competition is fierce and the training grueling, but that's the price of success in these sports.

Peggy Fleming of the United States skated to the gold with unmatched gracefulness in the 1968 Winter Games at Grenoble.

Training

THE PRINCIPLE OF SPECIFICITY

Training must closely follow the requirements of the activity. This is called the *principle of specificity* — the cornerstone of training for sports. If a sprinter were to overindulge in distance running, for example, he or she would lose the ability to move rapidly. As a sports physiologist, I feel that the Olympic Games have become so competitive in recent years largely because of a greater understanding of the principle of specificity in training. Athletes and coaches have been able to train harder and more effectively because of it.

One reason the decathlon is the glamour event in the Olympics is that it demands virtuoso handling of the principle of specificity. The decathlon gold medalist, hailed as the greatest physical specimen at the Games, must be an all-around athlete; success requires a balance of training for each of the ten events. If a decathlete develops too much strength and bulk, for example, his performance in the endurance and sprint events will suffer. Likewise, too much emphasis on endurance training will result in loss of points in the sprinting, throwing, and jumping events.

Top U.S. sprinters near the tape. Left to right: William Snoddy, Steve Riddick, Mike Miller, Steve Williams

One decathlete told me, "I was able to drop my 1,500-meter time to 4:03 by running twelve miles a day; however, when I started to concentrate on the sprints, jumps, and throws, I could only manage a 4:38." This athlete was experiencing the great paradox of the decathlon; if you work too hard in one type of event, your performance in the other events will suffer.

I was able to study Bruce Jenner in my laboratory several months before he won the gold medal in the decathlon at Montreal in 1976. Jenner's basic athletic skills and physiological characteristics were extremely well balanced — he was excellent, yet not superior in the various areas of fitness. His endurance was good, but it was closer to that of a professional tennis or soccer player than to a distance runner's. Although he was strong, his strength was nothing compared to that of a weightlifter or shot-putter. In short, Jenner's fitness reflected the demands of his sport — the decathlon requires a balance between strength, speed, endurance, and flexibility.

STRENGTH AND POWER

Sports scientists have made tremendous progress in understanding the role of muscle tissue in athletic performance. Techniques have been developed to help athletes choose the right event, and new training methods enable them to maximize strength and power.

One new technique that has greatly increased the understanding of the way muscles work is the muscle biopsy, a surgical procedure that allows scientists to obtain muscle samples. Muscle fibers are specialized: some contract rapidly, while others have more endurance. Speed in athletics requires a predominance of *fast-twitch* muscle fibers; endurance demands a predominance of *slow-twitch* muscle fibers. Sprint runners, for example, have more fast-twitch muscle fibers, and distance runners have more slow-twitch fibers. An athlete is probably born with a fixed ratio of fast- and slow-twitch muscle fibers. Early identification of fiber type, either by biopsy or non-surgical procedures, may prove valuable in some sports in the early selection of naturally gifted athletes. The old saying that sprinters are born and not made is true — if you aren't born with enough fast-twitch muscle fibers, you won't break the world record in the 100-meter dash.

Scientists have identified the predominant fiber types in many kinds of athletes:

Sport	Percentage of slow-twich muscle fibers	Percentage of fast-twitch muscle fibers
800-Meter Run	45	55
Sprinting	62	38
Marathon	82	18
Swimming	75	25
Cycling	58	42
Downhill Skiing	48	52
Discus Throw	48	52
Sedentary Population	48	52

These values represent the average — some sprinters, for example, have many more fast-twitch fibers than indicated on the chart. A fixed ratio of fiber type is not absolutely necessary for success, but it helps in many sports.

Weight training is practiced by many athletes and has accounted for the recent accelerated performances in sports such as swimming and track and field. In 1976, the East German women's swim team dominated the Olympics largely because of a vigorous weight-training program that had been incorporated into their regimen. But with the new emphasis on strength training in the United States, American women have regained their supremacy in swimming. Top Olympic prospect Libby Hill said, "Strength training has definitely turned around the fortunes of our women swimmers." Her comment is evidenced by the new world records recently set by Linda Jazek (backstroke) and young Mary Magher (200-meter butterfly), among others. Studies have shown that women are more efficient in the water than men, but can't swim as fast because they aren't as strong; however, continued emphasis on strength training for women will narrow the performance gap between the sexes and escalate Olympic competition even further.

Ken Stadel, powerful U.S. discus thrower, placed second in the 1979 AAU National Championship meet.

U.S. javelin thrower Kate Schmidt, perhaps the world's strongest female in her sport, won the bronze medal in the 1972 Olympics and again in 1976.

Weight training has been particularly important in the throwing events of the Games. In the shot-put competition at the 1948 Olympiad in London, at a time when weight training was not stressed, the winning throw was 56 feet-2 inches. But in 1972 at Munich, a put of 68 feet-7½ inches captured only sixth place. Much of the increase in distance was due to an emphasis on weight training during the intervening years. Modern discus throwers must also be top-flight weightlifters. I remember seeing Al Oerter at the West Coast Relays just before the 1968 Olympics. He was powerful-looking from years of heavy weightlifting.

U.S. runner Madeline Manning copped the gold in the 800-meter race at Mexico City in 1968 with a time of 2 minutes-0.9 seconds.

U.S. race walker Neal Pyke strides past the competition in an AAU meet.

In 1979, as he geared up for the Moscow Games at the National Sports Festival in Colorado Springs, he looked awesome. He had to be: to produce Olympic-caliber performances more than ten years after his victory in 1968, Oerter needed much more strength than ever. He was bench-pressing about 460 pounds in 1968. In 1979, he pressed 540 pounds.

Newly developed strength-training methods will continue to improve performance in many sports. The most notable new methods are isokinetics and the Nautilus program. Isokinetics allows athletes to develop strength at high speeds of motion and thus is more specific to many movements used in sports. Nautilus training utilizes machines that isolate muscle groups and develop them throughout the full range of motion. This type of training is proving very valuable in sports where top performance depends on muscle endurance, such as swimming and wrestling.

Rising U.S. track star Mark Belger (center) accelerates in the 1,500-meter run at an AAU Championship meet.

ENDURANCE AND SPEED

Endurance is a critical fitness component in many sports and greatly contributes to the drama of the Olympics. Some of the most memorable

moments at the Games have occurred in events such as the 10,000-meter run, when athletes were driven to the end of their stamina to achieve great feats of courage and ability. Several factors contribute to the endurance capacity of the Olympians. The cardiovascular system of the top endurance athlete is almost like a fine racing car; it's built to work at peak performance under difficult conditions for an extended period of time. The cardiac output of endurance athletes is exceptionally high: their hearts are capable of pumping a great amount of blood. The average person has a cardiac output capacity of slightly over 20 liters per minute — normally the maximum amount of blood the heart can pump during exhaustive exercise. The cardiac output of endurance athletes such as distance runners and cross-country skiers has been measured at more than 35 liters per minute. These athletes have larger, more powerful hearts that are capable of expelling more blood per contraction than the heart of the average person.

Olympic-caliber athletes also have more efficient chemical systems within their muscles. Chemicals called *enzymes* are very important for converting fuels such as fat and sugar into energy to do work. Athletes have extremely well developed enzyme systems; they also have better-developed blood supplies to the muscles, enabling oxygen to quickly reach the areas doing the work. The energy centers of cells are called *mitochondria*. Endurance athletes have larger and more numerous mitochondria, which supply a great amount of energy for exercise. In addition, these athletes have a larger percentage of slow-twitch muscle fibers, which are very well adapted to endurance work.

One of the most important factors in endurance performance is the athlete's maximal oxygen consumption capacity, called *VO_2 Max* by exercise physiologists. An athlete's maximal oxygen consumption level reflects the endurance requirements of his or her sport. The marathon demands a great deal of endurance, for example, while the discus throw requires relatively little. The decathlon falls somewhere in between.

Sports scientists typically determine maximal oxygen consumption capacity on a treadmill, stationary bicycle, or swimming flume (a swimming "treadmill"). The specific type of endurance required in specialized sports, such as rowing and cross-country skiing, is measured by special devices that have been recently developed. In the VO_2 Max test, an athlete's exercise capacity is determined through a work task that becomes more difficult with time. During the test, the expired breath is analyzed by high-speed instruments that instantly assess the capacity of the body's metabolism. These tests can be used to evaluate endurance potential, state of fitness, and proper training intensity, and are currently being administered to potential Olympians at the United States Olympic training centers in the hope of improving their performance.

The treadmill test determines an athlete's maximal oxygen consumption capacity, a critical factor in endurance performance.

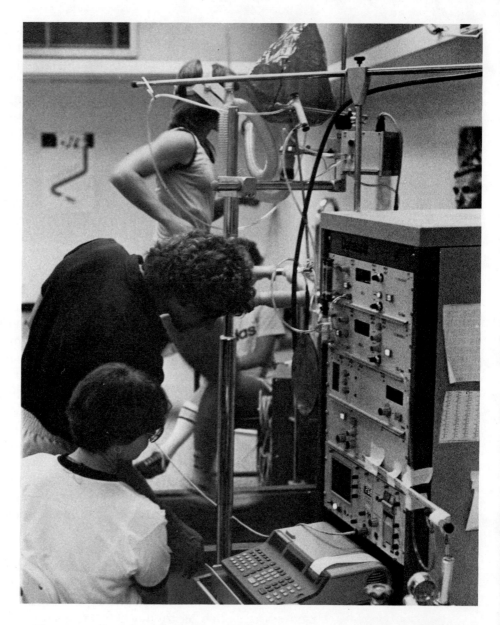

The average 25-year-old male has a maximal oxygen consumption capacity of about 40 to 45 milliliters of oxygen per kilogram of body weight. This compares with selected Olympic athletes as follows:

- Frank Shorter (marathon) — 85 milliliters per kilogram

- Bruce Jenner (decathlon) — 62 milliliters per kilogram

- John Powell (discus) — 52 milliliters per kilogram

To become a world-class distance runner, a male athlete must start with a maximal oxygen consumption capacity of at least 65 milliliters per kilogram of body weight; a female athlete needs about 55 milliliters per kilogram. Swimmers require a little less because the heart doesn't transport as much blood (and thus oxygen) when the body is in a supine position. An athlete can only expect to improve his or her endurance through training by about 20 percent. The purpose of endurance training is to improve maximal oxygen consumption and increase the length of time an athlete can work at a high percentage of maximum performance. Top endurance athletes are born with a high endurance capacity and then work extremely hard to develop themselves into world-class competitors. Improving endurance by a mere 1 or 2 percent can take years at that level. An aspiring athlete with only average stamina can never hope to achieve championship performance in endurance events; although it may be possible to improve the body's endurance through training, the gold medal will always be out of reach.

Endurance training has become both increasingly sophisticated and grueling. Fifty years ago, coaches believed that excessive training would burn out an athlete — former Stanford track coach Dink Templeton was considered a heretic in the 1930s and '40s for his belief that an athlete couldn't get enough work. Now endurance athletes put in incredible mileage. Because of the time and involvement necessary to develop top condition, training for endurance sports today is a full-time job.

Swimmers train anywhere from 10,000 to as much as 20,000 meters a day, all year long. It's quite a sight to see the steam rising from the pool in the dead of winter at six o'clock in the morning as young Olympic hopefuls do their morning workout. These young athletes will spend at least four hours in the water five or six days a week. They will supplement their swimming with weight training and, occasionally, distance running. To the international-class swimmer, the day of the competition is almost like a day off.

The life of the distance runner, race walker, or cross-country skier is similar to that of the swimmer. The distance runner will put in between 70 to 150 miles a week, depending on the time of year. During the noncompetitive season, emphasis is placed on overdistance, or long runs. However, during the early and active competitive seasons, the runner will concentrate on developing speed for the winning edge. Speed is important, even for distance athletes. Typically, a runner will develop speed with interval training — rapidly running short distances, usually between 100 and 1,320 yards, with a short rest period between repetitions. Interval training develops the metabolism for endurance and for the sudden bursts of speed that make the track events so exciting in the Olympics. However, the work is exhausting and often increases risk of injury.

In 1976, U.S. swimmer Mike Bruner snared the gold medal in the 200-meter butterfly with a time of 1 minute-59.23 seconds, an Olympic record.

Sports scientists have developed techniques to help athletes perform their intervals at the optimum pace and insure the fastest rate of improvement while minimizing the risk of injury. One such technique identifies the ideal training level. In the laboratory, the athlete performs a series of runs or swims at different speeds. Blood is taken from the earlobe and analyzed for lactic acid (a product of the breakdown of glucose, a simple sugar) after each bout of exercise. At high work loads, lactic acid increases with the intensity of exercise. High levels of lactic acid make recovery from repeated interval training more difficult; as a result, the total amount of exercise an athlete can perform in a workout is cut down. In addition, the training intensity associated with extremely high levels of lactic acid increases the risk of injury. With this test, the exercise physiologist can establish the training pace that will produce the ideal level of lactic acid. Gradually, the athlete can increase the intensity of training and systematically improve performance.

INJURIES AND THE PROSPECT OF SUCCESS

The Olympian lives with pain and injury. Training is an attempt to push the body just a little further than before — the body either adjusts and becomes stronger or it breaks down. The successful athlete knows when to back off from training, as well as when to surge ahead.

Throughout the history of the Olympics, injury has resulted in the downfall of many athletes. In the decathlon alone, the result of competition has often been decided by an athlete's ability to overcome injury. In

Sergei Vaitsehovsky, head coach of the Soviet swim team

Soaring young stars in the U.S. women's discus throw: Christy Pyle (right) and Julie Hansen (above)

1956 at Melbourne, the favored Rafer Johnson, competing with a bad knee and a pulled stomach muscle, lost to Milt Campbell. In a turnabout in Rome in 1960, Johnson edged out the injured Chuan Kwang Yang for the gold. In 1968, world record holder Kurt Bendlin was favored to win the javelin competition in the decathlon. But because of an elbow injury that caused him to double up in pain when he made his throw, Bendlin lost the chance of a lifetime to peg the gold and settled for a third-place finish instead.

Injuries have created a field day for the "what-ifers": What if Don Quarrie (200-meter dash, ranked first in 1971) hadn't pulled a muscle coming out of the turn during the semi-finals in 1972 at Munich? Would Quarrie have beaten Silvio Leonard in the 200-meter run in 1976 if Leonard hadn't had a severely cut foot? What if the great miler Jim Ryun hadn't contracted mononucleosis before his aborted attempt at the gold medal in the 1,500-meter run at Mexico City in 1968? Injuries and illness have ruined the careers of many great athletes, and have certainly affected the outcome of many contests at the Games.

The training required for success in the Olympics goes hand in hand with a great risk of injuries. In swimming, for example, athletes have almost doubled the distance swum in a workout in the last ten years, but one consequence has been a number of shoulder injuries that have hampered performance. In the middle-distance events in track and field, such as the 800- and 1,500-meter runs, renewed emphasis has been placed on high-intensity interval training, and this has drastically increased the incidence of injury. Weightlifting workouts, too, are placing more and more emphasis on maximum effort, which can overwhelm muscles and tendons. The Olympian today must walk the razor-fine line between success and disaster.

Ergogenic Aids

Ergogenic aids are substances that improve athletic performance. Throughout history, man has used a variety of potions in an attempt to enhance physical capacity. Because of the highly competitive nature of the Olympic Games and international competition in general, the idea of using a substance that provides an added edge becomes very attractive. Agents that can possibly aid performance, such as anabolic steroids and amphetamines, are banned from the Olympics. However, athletes often attempt to circumvent the rules. Other techniques, such as blood doping, are difficult to detect, and Olympic officials can do little to prevent their use in the Games.

"Unless you are exceptionally big, fast, and strong, you can't be competitive in throwing events without taking anabolic steroids," said a world-class shot-putter. Almost all the athletes in strength events such as weightlifting, discus throw, shot put, and hammer throw take these drugs in an attempt to become bigger and stronger. Anabolic steroids are synthetic male hormones. They have been manufactured to enhance the muscle-building properties of the hormones, with minimal effects on sexual characteristics. These drugs, known by such names as Dianabol, Winstrol, and Deca-durabolin, are most effective when taken in conjunction with protein supplements and accompanied by heavy weight-training. In research conducted at the DeAnza Lab, we found that anabolic steroids had little effect on the fitness characteristics of the average person. However, the athlete provides another story. Because of the incredible training loads of these people, steroids are very effective for increasing strength and muscle bulk. There have been few controlled studies of the effects of these drugs on world-class athletes. However, my personal observations of some of the best in the world make me conclude that they do make a difference in athletic performance.

Athletes were first tested for steroid use in 1976. The tests undoubtedly affected the competition at the Games — there was a noticeable decrease in the shot-put performances, for example, compared to the marks of the previous year and those of the Munich Olympics. In 1972, the winning put was 69 feet-6 inches, with sixth place at 68 feet-7$\frac{1}{4}$ inches. However, in 1976 the winning put was only 69 feet-$\frac{3}{4}$ inches, with sixth place at 66 feet-9$\frac{1}{2}$ inches. The distance of the puts was significantly less at Montreal (for the first time in Olympic history), even though there had been a tremendous increase in the overall quality of performances in the years between Olympics; prior to the 1976 Games, no fewer than five athletes had thrown over 70 feet. Most athletes,

Bart Conner, stellar U.S. gymnast, racks up points on the parallel bars.

fearing detection, stopped taking the steroids two to six weeks before the Games and their performances suffered. Anabolic steroids are stored in the body fat, so they can still be detected for some time after the actual administration of the drug has ceased. For this reason, the athlete's percentage of body fat will determine the layoff needed to avoid detection in the Olympics. Although the steroid tests in 1976 were common knowledge, several athletes were detected and subsequently disqualified.

Detection of anabolic steroids in the body is complicated and expensive. The urine of the athletes is analyzed by two methods: mass spectrometry and radioimmunoassay. Mass spectrometry detects the differences in molecular weight of substances in the urine. Radioimmunoassay is a chemical procedure involving radioactively tagged hormones.

Blood tests are considered more precise, but aren't used in the Olympic Games at present.

Anabolic steroids can have a remarkable effect on the performance of women athletes in most sports. Male hormones account for much of the difference in performance and strength between men and women; levels of testosterone are about ten times higher in men than in women (600 vs. 60 nanograms of testosterone per 100 milliliters of blood). Although anabolic steroids can cause rather severe side effects in female athletes, such as masculinization and hormonal disturbances, they result in a tremendously unfair advantage in women's competition. A female athlete taking these drugs can expect to gain strength, speed, power, and size (and perhaps a beard) at a much faster rate than normal training would allow.

Do some women athletes use anabolic steroids? Many coaches assume that the East German women's swim team, for example, were probably given anabolic steroids — their tremendous musculature was much more than could be expected from weight training alone. In addition, a defector from that team charged that the women swimmers were given the drugs under the guise of vitamin pills. But there was no proof. However, when Finland and Russia competed in a women's cross-country ski race, knowledgeable sources reported that the use of steroids was detected in the entire Russian team. Despite an agreement between the Russians and Finns to test athletes only for amphetamines, the Finns tested their opponents for steroids in addition. Because of the agreement, no one was disqualified and the incident was hushed up. Yet this was the first definite indication of the use of anabolic steroids by Communist athletes. And in October 1979, seven East European women track and field stars were banned indefinitely from international competition for failing drug tests made at summer meets that year.

Waiting to compete

Another ergogenic aid that has been the focus of much speculation in the recent Olympics is blood doping, a technique that involves transfusing the athlete's own stored blood shortly before the competition. This practice was described in an article by Bjorn Ekblom of Sweden that appeared in the *Journal of Applied Physiology*. In Ekblom's experiment, a liter of blood was extracted from each of his subjects and stored for a month. During that time, each athlete's blood supply replenished back to normal levels. Then, the liter of stored blood was reinfused. The results were startling: maximal oxygen consumption improved by 12 percent and work capacity by 25 percent. Although these findings stirred up controversy among exercise physiologists, in theory blood doping has great appeal as an ergogenic aid.

It has been charged that Lasse Viren used blood doping to help him win his long-distance runs in the Olympics. Viren almost disappears from the face of the earth between each Olympiad, only to surface every four years and dominate the competition. The blood doping charges are, I feel, unfair. Viren was injured for much of the time between 1972 and 1976, yet the marks he turned in during those years were world-class — they just didn't receive any publicity.

Athletes use many other stamina-enhancing agents in the hope of optimizing performance. Vitamins are undoubtedly the most popular form

U.S. Olympian Jane Frederick placed seventh in the pentathlon at Montreal, and has fared well in major competition since then. Here she demonstrates her Olympic form in the shot put and the long jump.

of dietary supplementation. The typical athlete's medicine cabinet is crammed with a potpourri of pills ranging from vitamin C tablets to bee pollen. Scientific research indicates that most of these are a waste of money. However, the metabolism of the trained athlete cannot be compared with that of the sedentary subjects used in most nutritional research. I think the effectiveness of many of the dietary supplements that athletes consume remains to be adequately evaluated.

Tracee Talavera

Christa Canary

Rhonda Schwandt

Chris Riegel

Barbie Myslack

Ann Carr

Donna Turnbow

3
THE MIND

My victory at the Montreal Olympics didn't surprise me because I had won the gold medal in my mind thousands of times," said Bruce Jenner. "When I stepped out on the track or looked down the pole-vault runway, I felt comfortable because I'd been there before. During practice in the previous year I imagined myself in the Olympic stadium everytime I picked up a discus or threw the javelin. The Games themselves were nothing more than living out something I'd already done. I used to dream about my performance — I knew what it was going to feel like. That day the idea of failing never even occurred to me. I knew I was going to win: it was my destiny. I had made it that way."

Jenner said that once an athlete reaches the Games, success is 80 percent mental and only 20 percent physical. "You have to be physically prepared to be in the Olympics — you wouldn't be there if you weren't. In most events, any of the finalists has a shot at the gold. The winner will be the one who keeps his head, the one with the most mental toughness. There are incredible pressures at the Olympics. The great champion can get the pressure to work *for* him instead of against him."

The Winning Edge

The Olympics are the ultimate athletic proving grounds of the human being. The competition brings together exquisitely prepared men and women in a pressure-cooker atmosphere. All of them are trying for the same thing: victory. The winners will be those who are best prepared both physically and mentally. The line between success and failure is sometimes no more than a hundredth of a second or a few millimeters. The great champion always seems to give that little extra that achieves the margin of victory, no matter how small it may be. Olympic immortals such as Jenner, Al Oerter, Jean-Claude Killy, Donna deVarona, and Jesse Owens have that special "something" that sets them apart and makes them great. What are these mysterious ingredients that constitute a winner? Why is it that a person who may hold the world record and completely dominate an event or sport will sometimes fold in the Olympics — while another person, perhaps injured and less physically skilled, will rise up in the Games for a great victory?

Francie Larrieu, top U.S. distance runner

Brendan Foster, bronze medalist in the 1976 10,000-meter run, may have shed some light on a critical prerequisite of the champion when he said, "It seems to me that about six or so athletes at the Olympic starting line have good chances; but out of those six, one knows he is going to win. And there's a big difference between wanting to win and knowing you will win." Merely making the Olympic team requires a tremendous drive and single-minded dedication to one's sport. The great champion must exhibit exceptional mettle in the company of so many tough-minded competitors.

Successful American amateur athletes are criticized in some circles because of their lifestyles: total devotion to their sport often signals an expense to their careers, their family and, in some instances, their health. Yet this lifestyle is the inevitable consequence of the requirements of world-class performance. Olympic competition is so severe that to become complacent will mean the loss of the chance to compete. Bruce Jenner said to me, "I was on the road to victory when I realized I had to give up everything for the decathlon. Before my enlightenment, my progress was not as rapid and my performances were uneven. Once I got going, I would have moved into a cave and become a hermit if that's what it took to win. I would have done anything for my gold medal."

Much of the appeal of sports stems from the fact that athletes are forced to face the Moment of Truth. Sports place success and failure directly before the public eye; in few endeavors of life is achievement — or lack of it — so blatantly visible. This kind of environment demands a realistic perspective, and will eventually weed out aspiring athletes who may be unable to face the truth about their limited abilities.

U.S. long-jumper Bob Beamon digs into the sand pit after a record-shattering leap of 29 feet-2½ inches in his first attempt at Mexico City. Beamon's feat still stands as the world record.

Austrian gold medalist Franz Klammer clocked a breathtaking 1 minute-45.73 seconds in the downhill race at Innsbruck, 1976.

A great part of the attraction of the Olympics is the tremendous mental agility and courage consistently exhibited at the Games. Great champions are able to produce clutch performances when the chips are down. It was no accident that Bob Beamon produced his great long jump of 29 feet-2½ inches in the 1968 Olympic Games — he was a champion. Beamon's jump, perhaps the greatest athletic feat in history, could have occurred in any of a score of meets that he entered during his career. But it did not. The jump came in the Big Meet, when the pressure was on. That ability to produce a top performance when it counts most is the mark of a true champion. The world remembers Franz Klammer's death-defying downhill victory at 1976 Winter Games because it occurred in the Olympics. Other skiers may have superior records, but Klammer will be remembered because he produced in the big one. All eyes are on the Olympians; the pressure is awesome. To perform well under such circumstances takes tremendous mental fortitude.

The Psychology of Olympic Form

Psychologist Thomas Tutko of San Jose State University has called top-caliber sports the "P.T.A. Club" — for Pain, Tears, and Agony. Yet sports psychologists have studied successful athletes in great detail and have found, with a few remarkable exceptions, that Olympians are characterized by extreme emotional stability. The survival-of-the-fittest atmosphere of the Olympics, coupled with the physically exhausting training and the requisite psychological perspective of sports at this level, demands a great degree of mental and emotional toughness even to participate.

Dr. Bruce Ogilvie, perhaps the best-known sports psychologist in the world, described the mental and emotional character of the Olympic-caliber athlete: "Successful athletes are achievement-oriented people who derive personal satisfaction from striving. High achievement needs are based upon personal attitudes about the probability of success or failure associated with each investment of self or ego. All things considered, the outstanding athlete is at his very best when the odds are slightly against him. Ambitious people derive slight joy, if any, when their ability remains uncontested. The great athletes I have interviewed do not dwell upon their losses but concentrate on that part of their performance that limits their excellence.

"Olympians have a great need to be on top, and show as a group an exceedingly high need to be successful", Dr. Ogilvie continued. "They have a greater need for freedom and self-direction, preferring to make their own judgments as to what's good for them. They have a greater need for the spotlight than the average person and enjoy receiving more attention and acclaim. Olympians seem to have an easier time expressing aggressive tendencies and standing up for what they believe — they have a greater tendency to fight for their point of view. Their ability to engage in abstract thinking placed them in the upper 15 percent of the population. Olympians also have a greater awareness of reality; they call a spade a spade."

Sports scientists have noted few psychological differences between male and female athletes. Women in sports tend to be less dominant than men, but more impulsive, more aware of danger, more apt to punish themselves when they lose, and more concerned with other people. These differences may stem from pressures on women athletes, however subtle, to conform to traditional ideas of femininity. The "winning-at-all-cost" philosophy of males is considered unfeminine by many segments of our society. ("Women aren't supposed to sweat and get strong.") Although opportunities for women in sports are improving, culturally defined role models of masculinity and femininity are slow to change. Any pressures that are rooted in these traditionalist roles can

Jan Merrill set an American record in the 1,500-meter run with a time of 4 minutes-2.61 seconds in the semifinals at Montreal.

exert many negative effects on female athletes by increasing the odds against success in top-level competition.

In *The Young Athlete* (Bull Publishing, 1979), Dr. Ogilvie shows that the character traits of typical female athletes set them apart from most average women: "They need and seek high goals and high achievement. They have strong desires to accomplish something of significance. They thrive on being in the spotlight, and enjoy being in the center of attention. They have a strongly developed sense of independence and autonomy, and the ability to express aggression without feeling guilt.... Such women tend to be tough-minded, self-assured, self-confident, very trusting and self-assertive. They measure slightly above average in terms of emotional maturity, and rarely experience feelings of depression." In general, the character profiles of successful female athletes are remarkably similar to those of their male counterparts.

Most studies by sports psychologists indicate that there is little difference in character profile among athletes in various sports. There are exceptions. Runners and race walkers tend to be more introverted and more insecure. Stories of sub-4-minute miler Jim Ryun, for example, show an athlete with lapses in confidence — particularly during the early stages of his career. Dr. Bruce Ogilvie has, however, identified differences in character between medal winners and non-medal winners. Probably the greatest quality unique to medalists is that they're almost completely free of physical fear. This trait has obvious benefits for the champion. Breaking the pain threshold is usually associated with top performance — the winner has the ability to maximize his or her ability by teetering on the brink of disaster.

Dr. Ogilvie found that Olympic medal winners were different in other ways: medalists were more independent, less inclined to want to be members of a group, more self-reliant and self-disciplined, and more ambitious. Many medalists are stimulus addicts — they have a much greater need to bring change into their lives with new and different experiences. This trait is very important, particularly for younger, less experienced athletes, because it enables them to achieve one goal and immediately set a new, higher one. Making the Olympic team, for example, can be a great shock in itself; from there, the athlete must adjust his or her goal to winning a medal.

Other athletes showing deviations from the norm are those in high-risk sports, such as Alpine skiers who plummet down icy mountainsides at speeds exceeding 75 miles per hour. These athletes excel in tests of abstract reasoning. They can derive a form of psychic ecstasy by tempting fate during sports. They are very much aware of the risks they take. Often these athletes are loners, but they are also leaders and expect to be treated as such. In general, they are very together people.

Bob Bonderant, coach of many great racing car drivers, recently de-

Liudmila Turischeva took the all-around individual gold in women's gymnastics at Munich, and two silver medals and a bronze at Montreal. She anchored the team gold medal for Russia at both those Olympiads.

scribed the motivation to excel in one of his new students, Bruce Jenner, who was attending Bonderant's famous racing school at Sear's Point Raceway in California in preparation for a celebrity auto race. "Jenner has the ability to push himself to the maximum of his abilities," Bonderant said. "Sure, he has a long way to go to be a top race driver, but he uses everything he has to get the most from his car. I think if he stuck with it he could have great success in this sport."

THE STRESS FACTOR

There is little evidence to suggest that participation in high-level athletic competition can actually benefit mental health — most athletes are emotionally stable because they entered sports that way in the first place. Athletes have to be psychologically sound to survive the pressures of high-level sports, but the stress of competition can sometimes be overpowering. "About 40 to 50 percent of Olympic athletes feel stress they have trouble dealing with," said Dr. Ogilvie, "stress that can affect their performance. The psychologist can sometimes help the athlete deal with stress and anxiety and enable him or her to reach full potential."

In a few rare instances, athletes can achieve tremendous success in spite of severe psychological problems. Dr. Ogilvie remembers one Olympic gold medalist who was referred to his clinic by the national team coach: "The athlete was described as emotionally confused, with highly variable performance and practice times, and an increased tendency toward social isolation. He was also subject to increased moodiness and periods of depression. There were times when he was so distracted that those around him thought he was out of contact with reality. The psychopathological signs were such that it seemed inconceivable that he had been one of the world's best athletes in his sport. His psychological profile was consistent with that of individuals who had been institutionalized."

Dr. Ogilvie described the athlete as prepsychotic, paranoid, immature, and narcissistic. How did this athlete make it to the top of his sport? "He was significantly more achievement-oriented," Dr. Ogilvie said. "His need to gain recognition and acclaim for accomplishments reached the top of the scale. He had a great capacity to stay with things and see them through to their conclusion."

The athlete's motivation was actually a pathological desire for parental and social approval. During one therapy session he broke down, bending forward with tears flowing from his eyes, and cried out, "Daddy why can't you accept me? Why can't you love me?" This athlete coupled a misguided motivation with awesome physical talent, and reached the top. However, he was greatly in need of help.

In summing up this case, Dr. Ogilvie put his role as a sports psychologist in perspective: "We must not lose sight of the fact that people in sports are individuals first and athletes second. The quest for athletic excellence must never be at the expense of their emotional health. Also, we should not let accomplishment in sport become a disguise for personal growth."

Kurt Thomas, 1976 Olympic gymnast and 1978 World Games gold medalist, displays near-flawless technique on the horizontal bar and the parallel bars.

THE MIND OF THE OLYMPIAN AT WORK

AL OERTER: "I NEVER MAKE ANY EXCUSES"

Perhaps the best example of "raw psyche" exhibited at the Olympics has been consistently demonstrated by Al Oerter, four-time gold medal winner in the discus throw. Again and again, Oerter has shown the characteristics of a great champion in the face of near-impossible odds. At twenty years of age he beat Fortune Gordien at Melbourne, in 1956, with a throw of 184 feet-10 inches — even though Gordien had thrown almost 20 feet farther in practice during the week before the Games. A less tenacious athlete would have been overwhelmed by the competition. In 1960 at Rome, Oerter beat Rink Babka with a throw of 194 feet-2 inches, despite the fact that Babka had bested him in the Olympic trials and held the world record at the time.

Oerter's two most impressive victories came in Tokyo and in Mexico City. At Tokyo in 1964, he went into the games with a pinched nerve in his neck and torn cartilage in his ribs. In addition, he was going up against three athletes who were throwing as well or better than he — Ludvik Danek, Jay Silvester, and Dave Weill. Danek held the new world record at 211 feet-9½ inches; Silvester had thrown 215 feet in practice, and Weill, with his 6-foot-8-inch frame, was capable of a tremendous throw. In spite of agonizing pain and stiff competition, Oerter blasted a throw of 200 feet-1 inch that fell short of the world record, but set a new Olympic mark and won him a third gold medal.

The discus event at the Mexico City Games in 1968 gives us a good idea of the effects that a great champion can have on other competitors. Oerter didn't appear to have much of a chance: athletes were throwing the discus practically out of sight. Silvester had broken the world record with a throw of over 218 feet, and reportedly had a practice throw in Utah of over 240 feet. George Puce of Canada had one of the leading throws in the world with a mark of over 210 feet. (In May of 1968 at Reno, I was amazed to see Puce make five consecutive practice throws of over 220 feet.) It clearly looked like Oerter was washed up.

The competition at the Games was a discus thrower's nightmare. Rain caused the event to be delayed, making the circle slick and increasing the throwers' edginess. The conditions unnerved many of the competitors, but not Oerter. In the first round, Lothar Milde of East Germany led with a throw of 204 feet-10 inches; Oerter was third with a throw of slightly over 202 feet. By the end of the second round, Oerter had dropped to fourth place. He hardly looked like the great champion who had dominated the Olympic discus event for so long. Then he dropped

U.S. discus hurler Al Oerter unleashes the form that copped the gold medal in four successive Olympiads, 1956-1968.

the bomb: 212 feet-6 inches. The rest of the field wilted and died on the vine. The other athletes could only manage fouls and "pus-arm" throws — Oerter had completely demoralized his competition. Then, in his typical championship fashion, he produced two more throws farther than 210 feet. Oerter again broke the Olympic record and won an incredible fourth gold medal. To quote Jay Silvester, "When you throw against Al Oerter, you don't expect to win — you just hope."

I asked Oerter about the apparent downfall of his competitors at Mexico City after his big throw. He replied, "A Czechoslovakian psychologist said that I exerted mind control over the other guys in Mexico. That's not true — I don't play mental games. I prepare myself for the Games as best I can. I never make any excuses. If I have any weak points, I correct them. Once I'm at the Games, I just concentrate on doing the best I can — I don't worry about anything else."

Promising U.S. track prospect Don Paige, 1979 NCAA champion in the 800- and 1,500-meter runs

U.S. high-jumper Pam Spencer executes the Fosbury Flop (a backward flip over the bar), which has virtually replaced the straddle style of jumping among women as well as men.

Rosalyn Bryant, one of America's top sprinters, set a U.S. record in the 400-meter dash by clocking 50.62 seconds in the semifinals at Montreal. In the 1,600-meter relay finals, she fired the U.S. team to a world-record-breaking time of 3 minutes-22.81 seconds and a silver medal.

The statistics reinforce Oerter's competitiveness. Bert Nelson, editor of *Track and Field News*, reported a study of five top discus men who had competed in three or more Olympics: Fortune Gordien had a distance average of his best Olympic throws that was only 94.4 percent of the distance average of his best pre-Olympic marks each season; Jay Silvester's Olympic distance average was 95.1; Adolfo Consolini's 95.9 percent; and Ludvik Danek's 96.8 percent. But Oerter's Olympic distance average was 100.3 percent — *better* than his non-Olympic marks.

As we have seen, most of the great Olympic champions seem to have superior mental toughness and psychological characteristics that make them outstanding. Oerter's attitude was very similar to Bruce Jenner's: neither would settle for anything less than victory. Oerter himself gives us a glimpse at the psychology of a champion in an interview that appeared in Cordner Nelson's *Track and Field: The Great Ones* (Pelham Books, 1970): "Once in the Olympic Village you can't improve on your strength and speed. The only thing still possible is to improve your

Top British shot-putter Geoff Capes placed sixth in that event at the Montreal Olympiad.

U.S. Javelin thrower Bill Schmidt pegged the bronze medal in the 1972 Games.

Top-ranked U.S. sprinter Clancy Edwards

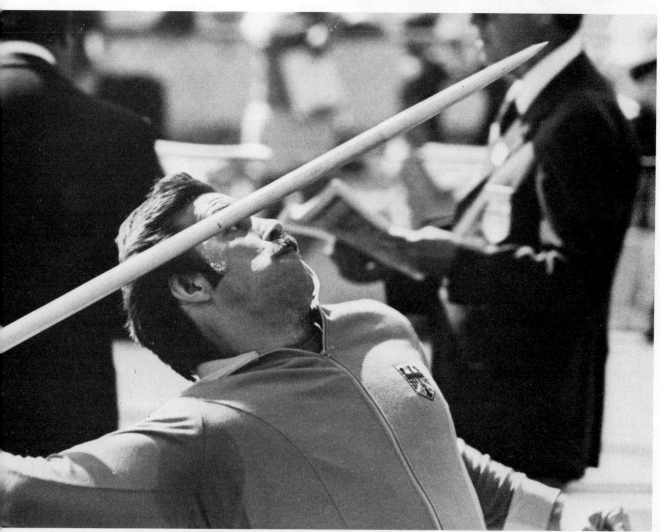

U.S. long-jumper
Martha Watson competed
in 1968 at Mexico City,
in 1972 at Munich, and
in 1976 at Montreal.

Daniel Bautista (left)
walked off with the gold
in the 20-kilometer race
at Montreal, while
Mexican teammate
Raul Gonzalez (right)
finished fifth.

mental attitude. In the weeks before an Olympic competition, I mentally simulate every conceivable situation for each throw. For example, I imagine I'm in eighth place, it's my fifth throw, and it's pouring rain. What do I do? An inexperienced thrower might panic or be thinking, 'I hope I don't fall down.' I know ahead of time what I will do under every condition.''

Recently, Oerter came out of retirement for a try at an unprecedented fifth gold medal at the Moscow Olympics in 1980. In 1979, at the age of 43, Oerter was throwing the discus farther than he ever did. Some of his marks exceed 219 feet. The great discus throwers of the world know that Oerter cannot be counted out of the competition — they have made that mistake before. They know that once Oerter gets close to the winner's circle, anything can happen.

LASSE VIREN: A HEAD WORTH GOLD

Lasse Viren, the great distance runner from Finland, has consistently exhibited extreme mental toughness in both the 1972 and 1976 Olympics. During the 10,000-meter run at the Munich Games, Viren stumbled and fell — the kiss of death in such a competitive field. Rather than quit,

Finnish distance runner Lasse Viren became the first man to win both the 5,000- and 10,000-meter races at successive Olympiads, 1972-1976.

he recovered and went on to win the gold medal, breaking the world record in the process.

Viren has won four gold medals at two Olympiads in spite of sometimes great controversy — which only magnified the pressure he was under. At Montreal in 1976, he was accused of blood doping, a technique to improve the ability of the blood to transport oxygen to the muscles (see page 85). And when Viren held his track shoes over his head after winning the 10,000-meter run, he was accused of illegally promoting the manufacturer. These charges put Viren under tremendous pressure and mental strain, yet he went on to win the gold medal in the 5,000-meter run and then placed fifth in the marathon just one day after that.

The characteristics that make Viren a winner are summarized by his doctor, Pekka Peltokallio, in the biography *Lasse Viren, Olympic Champion* by Raevuori Antero and Rolf Haikkola (Continental Publishing House, 1977): "Lasse has two golden gifts: his heart and his head.... Lasse's head is worth gold. By this I mean his strong psyche, but also his fighting spirit. On the track, he is like an animal in the hunt, listening to every little rustle. Running at the rear of the field and seeing a gap in front of him, he quickly occupies it. Somebody moves out, Lasse at once takes the vacant space near the curb of the track. He not only runs,

Viren (right) reaches the gold in the 5,000-meter race at Montreal. Dick Quax of New Zealand (#691) places second, and West Germany's Klaus Hildenbrand dives for third.

Top U.S. hurdler Patty Van Wolvelaere (right) receives some pointers and consolation from a coach.

but he senses, thinks, and maneuvers so cold-bloodedly that it is almost unbelievable. With eighty thousand people roaring all around him, he is not paralyzed; no, he is inspired."

Viren's character profile is similar to that of all the great champions: awesome physical talent and great physiological capacity, unbelievable mental toughness and self-confidence, and the ability to think and relax under pressure. Much of the ability the Olympian has is inborn. However, there are many instances when hard work and years of sacrifice have resulted in capabilities equal to those that other athletes are born with. Behavioral scientists are beginning to understand the psyche of the top competitive athlete. But perhaps the most enlightening insights of the mental prerequisites of Olympic competition are provided by the athletes themselves.

JOHN POWELL: THE ELEMENTS OF SUCCESS

The best description I've heard of the psychological factors necessary for Olympic success was made by John Powell, two-time Olympian, bronze medal winner in the discus throw, and former world record holder. Powell is an inspiration to aspiring young athletes because he has gone a long way on much less natural physical ability than his competitors. Through hard work and belief in himself, Powell has developed almost flawless technique and a reputation for coming up with a good performance when it's called for. He said, "The psychological tenacity necessary for success in sports can be broken down into three simple factors: belief, vision, and method. Belief is self-confidence — knowing your worth as an athlete and knowing you can do well. Vision is your goal — you have to know what you want in order to get it. Method is the process you use to fulfill your vision — how you train and how you handle yourself in the pressure and excitement of competition.''

Belief

"Belief," said Powell, "means having confidence in your abilities. Self-confidence is perhaps the most important mental attribute an athlete can have. If you don't have that, you will be nothing. Self-confidence takes a long time to develop; it's something you have to learn. Self-confidence is based on accomplishment, and it's developed by succeeding in a series of short-term goals. As you experience a number of small victories, you begin to realize that nothing is impossible. Then, the only thing to stop from getting what you want is yourself. If you don't believe you can do something, there's no way you will do it. Confidence or belief is the cornerstone of athletic success — or success in anything.''

Two-time U.S. Olympian John Powell, bronze medalist in the discus throw at Montreal: "Belief, vision, and method"

115

The importance of belief in sports is summed up by Don Schollander, gold medalist swimmer in the 1964 and 1968 games, in *Deep Water:* "In top competition where you are constantly up against unexpected situations and when every man is out for himself, confidence is important. Your competitor is out to get you any way that he can, short of foul play — and you are out to get him. You have to feel, absolutely, that you can take care of yourself, whatever happens, and you must have confidence in your own judgments — the courage, once you decide on strategy for a race, to stick to it. Without that kind of self-confidence you're vulnerable and your competitor will get you with a psyche-out or with his own race strategy, and you will lose."

The psychology of athletic competition is often very overt. Many athletic champions use intricate psychological tactics to thwart the self-confidence of their opponents. Schollander described one of these: "A psyche-out can be complex or simple. It can be worked a minute before the race or it can be continued carefully over several days. It can be directed against a single rival or against the entire field. The techniques vary, but the object is always the same: to convince your competition that you are certain to win the race. In a psyche-out you always make a show of confidence, while you work to undermine the confidence of your competition."

Few athletes are born with strong self-confidence and an iron-clad belief system. Rather, belief is part of a developing process that takes many years to mature. Jim Ryun, the great miler, recently reminisced about his first sub-4-minute mile (*Runner's World*, June 1979): "Coach Timmons and I had definite plans for me to become the first high school athlete to run under 4 minutes, but a couple of things were needed first. The main thing was I had to believe that it *was* possible, that I could do it. At the time, I had an incredibly poor self-image that had to be erased if I was to run a sub-4. Another thing I needed to make me believe I could run under 4 minutes was to run against older, more experienced runners." Ryun's belief crystallized when he had success against established runners. Then, as his self-confidence solidified, he could realistically focus his vision.

The coach can be instrumental in the athlete's development of self-confidence and vision. John Powell related his experiences with his high school coach: "When I started throwing the discus I had trouble staying on my high school track team; I never even thought about the world record or the Olympics. I had absolutely no confidence in my ability, but my coach did. He told me, 'I think you can throw five feet farther.' I didn't believe in myself but I believed in him, so I threw farther. I continued to improve in small steps, and my confidence grew. Soon, my goals became more stellar. But my goals and my vision were always realistic for the level of ability I was at. Realism will make or break your vision."

Don Schollander is the first to bang the finish wall in the 400-meter freestyle race at Tokyo in 1964 (right). He also won the 100-meter race and spurred his U.S. team to victory in two relays, becoming the first man ever to win four gold medals in Olympic swimming.

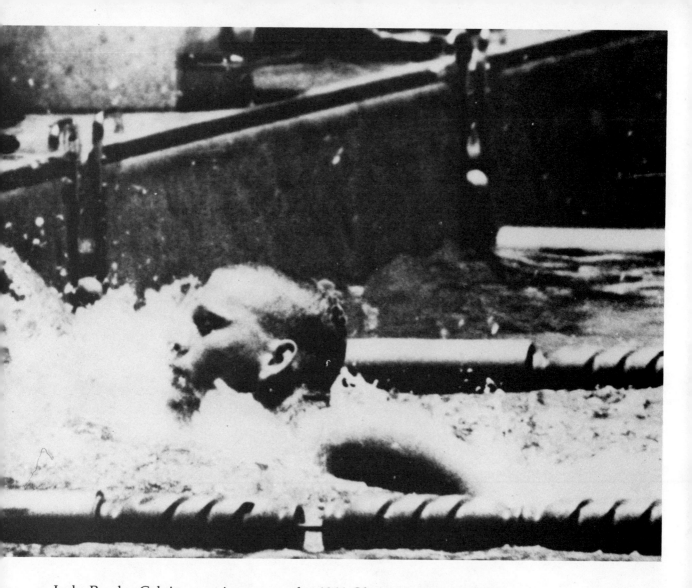

Judy Reeder-Calpin, a swimmer on the 1964 Olympic team, recently provided insights about the powers of the great coach George Haines, formerly of the Santa Clara Swim Club: "George Haines made each girl believe she could be a winner. He made each swimmer feel like he was her personal coach; we all loved him. In the Olympic trials, he inspired me. He told me I was going to win and I believed him. After that, I was not afraid and I wasn't worried about winning."

"Topper" Hagerman, director of the Sports Medicine Laboratory at the Olympic training center in Squaw Valley, feels that experience is the key to genuine self-confidence: "Experienced athletes can put athletics in their proper perspective. They know their capabilities better, and they are much better able to deal with pain. They become students of their sport and learn quite a bit about the theory behind training methods and about the physiology and psychology of athletics. All this combines to give them confidence. Younger or less experienced athletes are

OUTSTANDING
YOUNG
COMPETITORS IN
WOMEN'S
SWIMMING

Right: Larissa Tsarova,
Soviet Union (freestyle)

Linda Jezek, United States (backstroke)

Above: Donnalee Wennerstrom, United States (butterfly)

Right: Julia Bogdanova, Soviet Union (breaststroke)

usually not very confident because they don't give themselves long enough to learn the ropes."

Experienced athletes, almost without exception, seem to know themselves extremely well. In talking with scores of champions, I found that those who have been around for awhile are certainly more philosophical about their sport; they've had more time to think and learn about it. I am amazed to see the decidedly positive attitudes in all the great athletes I talked to. Most of them seem to believe they are capable of anything in almost any aspect of their life — not only in sports, but in whatever they might attempt. They are extreme optimists. They take pride in their abilities to control tremendous mental energy and pressure. Bruce Jenner described this ability as he applied it in the Montreal Games: "When I was in the blocks, I imagined myself one step out as the gun sounded. I wanted to let all of the tension I'd built up in my brain work for me and help me to explode!" The great Olympians can extend their belief and positive self-image into their performance — and win because of it.

Vision

Vision is knowing what you want to achieve. I've seen many potentially great athletes never make it because their vision wasn't strong enough. Vision, like self-confidence, takes a long time to develop; in fact, both go hand in hand. John Powell related a recent experience: "A young long-jumper told me that he was going to make the Olympic team and break the world record. He was jumping only 23 feet at the time. I asked him, 'Why don't you shoot for 23 feet-6 inches before dreaming about taking all the marbles?' He wasn't being realistic — that pie-in-the-sky stuff leads a lot of athletes into early retirement. He didn't realize that vision is built upon a series of small steps. As you learn your capabilities, you adjust your goals accordingly. I think it's important to enjoy the process of development. Reaching the Olympics is a hollow victory if you didn't enjoy the trip up."

Vision involves not only defining your goals, but accepting what is necessary to achieve them. Champions are often described as having a "killer instinct." That instinct may be the special something that provides that extra margin for victory. Whether this inner drive is inborn or inbred is not known; however, it is an important ingredient to vision.

Judy Reeder-Calpin described her college roommate, gold medal swimmer Donna deVarona: "Donna had that killer instinct, a desire to win and defeat opponents at all costs. She would not accept defeat in a race that was important to her. I think she wanted to win more than the

Rumanian gymnast Alina Goreac, a teammate of Nadia Comaneci

120

other girls, and that's why she was so good." Donna herself talked about the killer instinct: "My father said I was born with it. I would never settle for anything but the best. It's like with my present job in television — I am determined to be the best sportscaster, and I know I can do it."

In his autobiography *First Four Minutes*, sub-4-minute miler Roger Bannister described similar attributes in John Landy, the great miler from Australia: "Landy demonstrated a character capable of the greatest kindness, gentleness and thoughtfulness, and on the other side — as there always must be — a ruthless lack of feeling for others and a ferocity and antagonism, although it is mostly vented on himself, that makes it possible on occasions for John to rise to sublime heights of physical endeavor."

Bruce Jenner's gold medal victory in the decathlon at the 1976 Olympiad can perhaps be traced to the moment when he focused his vision: Jenner placed tenth in the 1972 Games and was confident that he could win in Montreal with four more years of training. His timetable continued to look good until 1975, when his improvement seemed to halt. "I started hedging my bets," said Jenner, "and worrying about what I

Britain's Roger Bannister (left) noses past Australia's John Landy in the final turn of the mile race at the Empire Games in 1954.

would do if I lost. I began to devote more time to my insurance business. Although I was training hard, I wasn't concentrating as much as I should have been.

"The combined trials for the National Championship and Pan-American Games looked like they might be my Waterloo. I just didn't have it together. The starting height in the pole vault was 14 feet, only 6 inches higher than I'd vaulted in high school. When I missed the height three times in a row, I was out of the competition. I lost control of myself: I threw the pole as hard as I could, almost taking the head off a nearby cameraman. I ran from the stadium, sat next to a tree and wept. Everything I'd worked for during eleven years was slipping through my fingers. My wife, Chrystie, came over to me and we had a soul-searching discussion that was to fix my resolve to win."

"Is the Olympic gold medal the most important thing in your life?" she asked.

"Of course it is," answered Bruce. However, as Bruce thought to himself he realized that he had been letting other things interfere with his vision. Sure, he was training hard, but he wasn't putting in that little extra effort it takes to improve consistently and win. "I was too concerned about what I would do if I lost," he admitted.

At that moment, Jenner decided that winning the Games was the most important thing in his life. Nothing was going to stand in his way. "If I lost, I would deal with that when it happened. I resolved to put aside anything that wasn't contributing to my vision of victory at Montreal. I gave up my job and devoted everything to the decathlon. I knew what I wanted, and I was going to get it."

During the early stages of an athlete's career, vision can come from a variety of places — parents, coaches, other athletes. However, the time must come when an athlete's goals are inner-motivated. The training is too hard, the competition too stiff, and the stress too great for anything but intrinsic incentive. A world-class athlete will seldom make it to the top because he's trying to win for his parents, coaches, and even for his country. These things may be factors in motivation, but in the end each athlete must want more than anything to succeed for himself or herself.

Method

Method is the process of achieving vision. Most people are familiar with the physical methods of athletics: obviously, a lot of hard work is necessary to achieve Olympic-level success. However, mental agility is also necessary for that kind of achievement. Efficient training programs, competitive tactics, an athlete's coachability, and his or her ability to employ psyching techniques are all part of the psychological category of athletics.

Gold medalist Jenner: "I knew what I wanted, and I was going to get it."

John Powell discussed method with me: "Self-confidence and vision mean nothing if you can't deliver the goods. Athletics are so competitive that to be successful, you have to use your practice time effectively. You can't leave anything to chance. I analyze every aspect of my technique and physical capacity. I try to maximize all the strengths I have. There are a lot of athletes who are much stronger than I, and the only way I can beat them is by having better technique and by being as fast as possible in the circle. Changing your technique, even by nuances, takes years; I will work on something until I've mastered it. I feel that I have the best technique of the world-class throwers — I have to because they're all bigger and stronger than I am.

"A lot of athletes aren't as successful as they could be because they don't think. They tend to work on their strong points rather than develop their weaknesses. I see some discus throwers who can bench-press almost 600 pounds concentrating on gaining upper-body strength when they should be working on their throwing. They have plenty of strength — what they need to do is work on their lousy technique."

The champion must be able to adjust to many conditions and employ many different strategies and methods of achieving the same end — victory. This ability was aptly described by Ron Clarke, one of the all-time great distance runners, in a profile published by *Track and Field News*: "The distance-running champion who sets a world record has to have a tough psychological approach to his running. The Olympic, European, and Commonwealth meets are harder to win than other meets because there are more people with similar ability who may just happen to click under the tactics you use. When you can concentrate on dropping off just three or four people in a race, you're almost certainly going to beat them. But when there are maybe a dozen people all around the same standard, your tactics to defeat three or four may not fit so many. This is what often happens in the big ones nowadays."

Method relates to belief and vision: the ability and daring to try certain strategies and tactics depends on an athlete's self-confidence and goals. In *First Four Minutes*, Roger Bannister shows this relationship as he describes a runner's decision to break from the pack and sprint to victory: "The decision to break away results from a mixture of confidence and lack of it. The breaker is confident to the extent that he suddenly decides the speed has become slower than he can himself sustain to the finish. Hence he can accelerate suddenly and maintain his new speed to the tape. But he also lacks confidence, feeling that unless he makes a move now, everyone else will do so and he will be left standing."

The champion seems to be able to get other athletes to subscribe to his game plan. A good example is the men's 1,500-meter race in the 1976 Olympics. At the time, the world record in the mile was 3 minutes-49.4 seconds, held by John Walker of New Zealand. But during the semi-

finals for the Games, 25 men had broken 3:40 in the 1,500-meter run, which is slightly less than a mile. In the 1,500 meter final, the athletes allowed the race to progress slowly, and then had to contend with Walker's kick and incredible speed when he decided to break away. Walker ran the final 400 meters in 52 seconds to capture the gold medal in the time, albeit relatively slow, of 3:39.17.

Belief, vision, and method are inseparable. Each is an essential ingredient in the formula for athletic success, and together they comprise the inner drive of the true champion. Although these character traits are hereditary to a degree, they can be developed to their fullest only through single-minded devotion to sports and perseverance — a lifetime of perseverance. In reality, athletic champions are no different from men and women who make great fortunes in the business world: athletes and professional people alike must have tremendous focus and tenacity to succeed. But while business offers the lure of money and power, in sports these are only secondary. The real reward of athletic excellence is less tangible. Even participation in a field of extraordinarily talented, intensely competitive athletes is a goal in itself. But for one athlete to weather the competition and rise to victory against all the opponents — that is something else again. Bruce Jenner described it best when he said that winning the decathlon brought him a special kind of satisfaction:

"It was everything."

Up-and-coming U.S. gymnast Mark Casso relaxes during a training break.

INDEX

Page entries in *italics* refer to illustrations.

THE MOST IMPORTANT
THING IN THE OLYMPIC
GAMES IS NOT TO WIN
BUT TO TAKE PART...

Edward M. Kennedy, Eunice Kennedy Shriver